BIG CREEK

A Closer Look at a National Park

Dinata Misovec

Hugo House Publishers, Ltd.

ISBN: 978-1-936449-89-7 (Trade Paperback)
Library of Congress Control Number: 2017940734

Book Cover and Interior Design: Christa E. Kegl

Hugo House Publishers, Ltd.
Englewood, Colorado
Austin, Texas
WWW.HugoHousePublishers.com

To Andy, who happily goes along with all my adventure schemes. Everyone should have a cheering section and support system as enthusiastic as he is.

Contents

Acknowledgements

I wrote the journals, but a number of people helped me turn them into a book.

Dana Soehn, the Great Smoky Mountains National Park Public Information Officer, provided information and referred me to park employees who could answer my questions. Can I thank a web site? Maybe not. However, the unknown people who create and maintain the excellent Great Smoky Mountains National Park web site are to be lauded for the wealth of information it provides.

Sue Meyer deserves an award for slogging through hundreds of pages of journals and attempting to turn them into something readable. And, Kathy Misovec pointed out inconsistencies and other glaring errors I should have caught sooner. Thanks to both of you.

A huge thank you to Sheila Ball, Dawn Laatz, and Joyce Peckman for pointing out grammar and punctuation errors that would have embarrassed and humiliated me if they had been published. I was embarrassed enough when they found them.

Preface

Sometimes a person gets a notion to do something before thinking it through. That's spontaneity. If you don't know anything about a subject or experience, you can jump right in and find out, firsthand. That approach might not be advisable for flying an airplane, or trekking to the North Pole, but most of our adventures are tame enough not to actually kill us. My husband Andy and I had no idea what we were getting into when we signed up to be volunteer campground hosts in The Great Smoky Mountains National Park. We had visited a number of the parks in our travels, but had never even heard of the Great Smokies. Life is a collection of experiences, and campground hosting looked like a good one to add to our collection.

Yep, it was an eye-opening experience. We learned a lot about the Smokies and national parks in general. I can sum it up by saying there is a lot more going on in a park than most park visitors realize. There is a small army of park employees, from park rangers to maintenance workers, striving to make our park experience safe and enjoyable. Park Service employees are dedicated and probably would not want to do anything else for a living. We learned about weather in the Smoky Mountains. It rains. A lot. And, we learned about the number and variety of park visitors, hikers, campers, and picnickers. I won't even attempt to summarize that here. Finally, by listening to the park radio all day, every day, we learned about all the surprising things that go on in a national park every day. Who knew?

Prologue

The Great Smoky Mountains National Park lies on the border between North Carolina and Tennessee. The Appalachian Trail runs through, and is the state line within, the park. And, even though I didn't know it existed, just about everyone else did. It is the most visited national park in the country with 10,712,674 visitors in 2015, more than number two (Grand Canyon at 5,520,736) and three (Rocky Mountain National Park at 4,155,916) combined. That record will be broken again in 2016, the centennial of the National Park Service.

This park is different from many other national parks in that it was not truly a wilderness set aside by the government like Yellowstone, the Grand Canyon, and Yosemite. The mountains were the homeland of the Cherokee. Then Europeans began to arrive in the 1700s. Generations of settlers had lived in the mountains before Congress authorized the park in 1926. Another thing setting it apart from other national parks is that there is no entrance fee. Highway 441, which crosses through the middle of the park, was the major road crossing the southern Appalachian Mountains, and part of the agreement with North Carolina and Tennessee was that travelers would not have to pay to use it. Another factor in the visitation numbers is that the park is located in the east and is easily accessible from several large population areas.

Once Congress authorized a park, additional money was raised and donated to purchase the land. John D. Rockefeller, Jr. donated $5 million, a large sum in the 1920s. It took years to buy the land, evict residents and close the logging operations. The park was officially established in 1934, during the Great Depression. The park benefitted from the Depression as it led to plenty of Civilian Conservation Corps and Works Progress Administration laborers to make improvements such as roads, trails, buildings, and campgrounds.

The park is the largest protected area east of the Mississippi River with 521,085.66 acres, or over 800 square miles. There are 384 miles of roads and over 800 miles of hiking trails. The ten developed campgrounds comprise 1,000 sites. The 100 backcountry sites accommodate more than 77,000 overnight visitors per year. There are over 2,000 miles of streams containing an abundance of waterfalls and cascades.

The stars of the park are the flora and fauna. There are over 1,500 kinds of flowering plants. Perhaps the most famous are the mountain laurel, rhododendron and flame azaleas blooming from May through July, depending on the elevation. There are 137 kinds of trees, 154 shrubs, 7 sub-shrubs, and 32 vines. For the mushroom fans, there are about 3,500 species of macro fungi and an untold number of micro fungi still waiting to be discovered.

There are 66 types of mammals, the most famous being the bears and elk. Birders come for the more than 200 species of birds. The park is also famous for fishing. The most sought after are trout, but there are 67 species of fish in the park's streams. Among the 39 kinds of reptiles, the Mountain Rattlesnake and the Copperhead are the most dangerous. The park is even known as the "salamander capital of the world." Because of this incredible biodiversity, the park has been recognized by the United Nations as an International Biosphere Reserve.

In addition to nature, the park has preserved more than ninety buildings representing the Southern Appalachian culture of the 1800s. Most of the structures are log homes and farm buildings. That preserved history has earned it a United Nations' designation as a World Heritage Site.

The two main entrances to the Great Smoky Mountains National Park are on US 441 in Gatlinburg, Tennessee and Cherokee, North Carolina. The approaches to both of these entrances are lined with motels, restaurants, t-shirt shops, and tourist attractions. Many families vacation in Gatlinburg and nearby Pigeon Forge and visit the park as a part of their vacation. Newfound Gap, half way across the park on US 441, is a popular stop and the parking lot is often crowded with tourists visiting the Rockefeller Memorial and the restrooms. Clingman's Dome is seven miles up a side road from Newfound Gap with a high observation tower and mountain views all around on a clear day. The Dome is at an elevation of 6,643 feet, the highest point in the park. Big Creek is far removed from all these places, at the northeast edge of the park.

The entrance to Big Creek is about two miles off Interstate 40. There is not a t-shirt shop, or much else for that matter, in sight. The one-lane dirt and gravel road into the park is carved into a steep mountainside. The horse camp, group camp, picnic area and tent campground are about a mile in. It is a small campground with only twelve tent sites.

1

Green Campground Hosts

We arrived in The Great Smoky Mountains National Park on July 2, 2010 at the Cosby Ranger Station on the Tennessee side of the park. Ranger Dennis Milligan was waiting to greet us. I was startled when he came out of the ranger station carrying a rifle and wearing a gun on his hip. My idea of a park ranger was someone leading a group through the forest and pointing out wildflowers.

I later learned that there is a whole array of park ranger classifications, from collecting fees at the gate to law enforcement. Pointing out wildflowers falls somewhere in between. Their law enforcement duties include routine traffic stops for speeding, driving under the influence, and missing tail lights. They respond to far too many motor vehicle accidents. In addition to policing the roads, the rangers also mount search and rescue missions for hurt, lost and missing park visitors. They respond to emergency medical situations, such as heart attacks and broken bones. Rangers also enforce laws against harming the parks resources: from taking or defacing rocks to harvesting ginseng to feeding the bears. While they are at it, they put out wildfires. If that is not enough, they also manage the ten campgrounds. And in their spare time they administer the VIP (Volunteer in Parks) program. That is an additional 3,000 people.

Ranger Dennis Milligan was fresh faced and slender, the park service version of a Boy Scout. Perhaps it is more a reflection of my age than his that I exclaimed to Andy, "He doesn't look more than sixteen!" In reality, he was probably in his late twenties. He was also exceedingly friendly and I forgot about the guns.

Ranger Dennis issued us radios, keys, shirts, and brochures and led us to our camp host site at the Big Creek Campground on the North Carolina side. The next day our supervisor, Ranger Tim Rand, came to meet us and spent about half the day with us going over paperwork, rules and regulations, and showing us the tent and horse campgrounds, and the unused ranger station. Then we were officially Campground Hosts.

Ranger Tim Rand, in his early thirties, was six-foot-four, with dark hair and a handsome, boyish face. I fell in love right away. He was always smiling and polite, the kind of man you would want for a son, or to marry your daughter. He approached campers with such cheerful good manners that he never appeared to be "the law," but was the "nice, friendly ranger." His mood never varied from laid-back friendly. He was definitely one of the law-enforcement variety though. I asked him about a tree near our campsite and he said he didn't know anything about the trees or the flowers.

Our biggest job was to monitor the twelve tent campsites to make sure people paid their camping fee and did not leave food unattended to attract bears. That included trash, coolers, and cooking utensils. We also asked them to keep their dogs on a leash at all times. On the weekends, we were to attempt to keep people from parking illegally, which Tim admitted was an impossible task. Finally, he told us our top responsibility was to have fun and our second job was to make sure everyone else had fun and stayed safe. That sounded like a pretty good job description to me.

Our first day on the job as Campground Hosts was July 4th. OMG!! We had been thrown into the fire of a holiday weekend.

We took a morning walk around the campground. There was food left out in nearly every campsite. Regulations are that no food, trash, coolers, or cooking utensils are to be left at the campsite when they are not in use. It is all to be locked inside the car along with the toiletries and anything else with a scent. The dogs were off leashes. We left courtesy notices at the campsites and reminded people about the leash rules.

A courtesy notice is a gentle reminder for violations, not a ticket. It is a bright orange/yellow card about four by nine inches. The common rules violations - food left out, trash on site, unattended pets, etc. - are printed on one side so all we needed to do was check them off. The reverse side has a silhouette of a bear's head and large print saying, "Garbage Kills Bears." And it does. Bears that are attracted to campground food become a nuisance and then a danger. At that point, they may be euthanized.

One man told us he was not worried about bears; he had a gun and bears are good to eat. Andy suggested that other campers did not have guns to defend themselves if he attracted bears with food left out. People unleashed their dogs as soon as we left the campground.

The first problem of the day was a dog bitten by a copperhead snake. The owner brought the dog to us for help. I called dispatch on the radio and Ranger Tabby looked up a veterinarian phone number for me. The man stood next to the RV where he could get a cell phone signal and called the vet. They said "bring him in." After he hung up, the man said, "What I really wanted was some country knowledge, like dunk his head in turpentine or something like that." He decided to take his dog back home to Knoxville and see if he got better. The man neglected to mention that his dog was not on a leash in the campsite when he was bitten, but was sniffing around in the forest.

By late morning there were cars parked everywhere. The small lot was full and people were parking along the one-lane road. We spent a good part of the afternoon trying to prevent people from parking along the narrow road and blocking emergency access. Big Creek has a day use area with picnic tables and a swimming hole in the creek. The Baxter Creek Trail and the Benton McKaye trails begin at the bridge over the creek. It is also the trailhead for the Big Creek Trail, which goes up to the Midnight Hole and Mouse Creek Falls, so there were always a lot of day visitors.

Spence, the maintenance man, came to say hello while we ate our lunch. With his east Tennessee hillbilly accent and strong opinions on many topics, it was apparent right away that he is a character.

Robert Spence is a native of Cosby, Tennessee, just across Mt. Cammerer from Big Creek. And, yes, I did say "it was apparent right away that he is a character" in my original log in 2010. Even though he said he was a hillbilly, it was also apparent that he was intelligent and quick witted. He was in his fifties, too slender, with long blonde/gray hair.

On our mid-afternoon campground tour, the food was all cleaned up. People leashed their dogs when they saw us coming. Word had gotten around about the snake bite and one campsite had one man dog-sitting four dogs on leashes.

- **We kept our two-way park radio on all the time and listened to talk about a terrible traffic accident somewhere in the park for most of the day. Four people were taken to area hospitals in ambulances and one was airlifted to a larger hospital in Knoxville, TN. Park roads were closed.**

Early in the evening, two men came up to our campsite to say they had a pick-up truck pulling a trailer parked down at the horse camp. They had been swimming in the Midnight Hole and could not start the truck. They were sure it was not the battery. I called dispatch and they ordered a tow truck. The men did not have a battery jumper cable so Andy offered to lend him ours and got the truck started. I called dispatch to cancel the tow truck. They were sure it was not the battery.

We had not expected the job to be so exhausting.

2

How Did We Get There?

In the spring of 2007, my husband Andy and I bought a small motorhome about twenty-four feet long. It's the kind of RV where the bed lies over the truck's cab (a Class C). It seemed just right for taking some extended summer trips and exploring the country.

We were living aboard our boat in the Florida Keys at the time and, being boaters, we thought the RV needed a name like a boat. Before he was a retiree, Andy had been a scientist/mathematician/engineer. He suggested we call our new home Stochastic, which means "random." It came from a graduate-level advanced statistics class Andy had taught, Stochastic Processes. But I have to tell you, its name is something of a misnomer. We do not travel in a random manner, which is my style. Andy plans daily routes and overnight stops long before a trip begins.

The first summer we owned Stochastic, we set out from Florida on a road trip, first stopping in several states to visit family. While driving out of the campground in Yosemite National Park one day, we chatted with the couple at the entrance gate. They told us they were park volunteers. It seemed like a fun thing to do and I tucked the idea into the back of my head for some time in the future. We took long summer road trips for the next few years and then decided to try our hand at campground hosting in a national park.

Come to find out, volunteering in national parks is huge. I logged onto the National Park Service web site and clicked on the "Volunteer" button. We had been to a number of national parks, so I chose the Great Smoky Mountains National Park to see something new. I checked out their web site and discovered that the Great Smoky Mountains National Park has ten campgrounds. There was a phone number to call the park's volunteer coordinator, which I did. Several campgrounds needed hosts for the summer, but I was too ignorant to pick one. I mentioned that Andy likes to swim and the pleasant woman, Dana Soehn, suggested Big Creek because it has a swimming hole. The park map on the website gave me no clue what it was like, but I could see it is in the northeast section of the park, just off Interstate 40 on the Tennessee-North Carolina border. I signed up for July and August.

Big Creek is a beautiful, if not an extraordinary, landscape in the Appalachian mountain range. After a one-mile drive up a one-lane dirt road in a narrow mountain valley, we parked our motorhome in a small clearing. The camp host site had water, electric, and sewer hook-ups. Once we set up, we had all the conveniences of home. Heck, we _were_ home – and we loved it. The maintained areas are attractive. Big Creek, tumbling over boulders down the mountain, is beautiful.

What makes it different from the many other mountain valleys is the steady stream of park visitors. There are twelve campsites in the tents-only campground, eight in the horse campground and a limit of 25 campers in the group site. Day visitors pour in all day long to picnic, swim in the creek, go to the Midnight Hole, ride their horses up the Big Creek Trail, or head out on a hike. It was quite the eye-opener to see how busy a little campground in the mountain forest can be, but listening to the park radio was the real shocker. Who knew there would be so many mishaps occurring in a national park every day? It was even more shocking to discover how busy we would be.

From my years of being a boater and our tradition of writing a log every evening, I continued to write of our travel experiences on land. The main purpose, for me anyway, was to remember. I wanted to include enough detail to relive the experience in the future when I spend more time in the rocking chair. A second purpose was to share my adventures with friends and family. I would send out the daily log to family and friends with pictures every evening in an email. The journal is filled with an excruciating amount of detail to show what each day was really like. Most nights the journal was a stream-of-consciousness sort of thing where I typed without thinking and without reading what I had committed to bits and bytes. Come to find out, they liked it—and then they told friends about it, and the list of followers grew. I started to get feedback: "I am traveling with you vicariously." Or "Write a book!"

A book sounded like too much effort to me. It is a lot of work to get from a journal to a book. Compare Lewis and Clark's journals to "Undaunted Courage." But here I am, finally sitting down and figuring out how to make all this writing ready for human consumption. Now I wonder whether I was even conscious when I wrote them. The pictures are nice. If you want to see what Big Creek and the Great Smoky Mountain National Park look like, I posted pictures every day. You can see them at http://bigcreekjournal.blogspot.com/.

19

Now, it is a book and is a glimpse into all that is wonderful, awful, smelly, stupid and stupendous about the Great Smoky Mountain National Park. I have come to be truly in awe of all that the national park system stands for—the greatness that lies within each and every one of us. But to leave it at that would be incomplete. For what I also found was that the national parks also bring out the simple joys of life: finding a new friend to sit with by the campfire, learning about a youth group wanting to help, searching for a lost dog or helping a hurt child. And as I think back through the pages of what I've written, maybe that really is what brings out the best part of us. To paraphrase what other authors have said before me, I hope you have as much fun reading it as I had living it.

On our next early morning trip around the campground, we found seven empty campsites, but no messes. Folks cleaned up well before they left. Another of our tasks was to report the number of campsite vacancies every morning. About 11:00, the park dispatcher called each campground in alphabetical order and we responded with our number.

Just as we came out into the campground parking lot, we found a young newlywed couple towing her mother's pop-up camper, which had a flat tire. They had driven all the way in from the interstate when they realized Big Creek is a tent-only campground. At that point, he had said, "Well that's the first thing to go wrong on this trip." Then he hit a rock and bent the wheel on the camper, letting the air out of the tire. They tried to open the camper to look for tire-changing tools and wasps swarmed out. Then they decided to use the vehicle tools to change the tire, but they did not fit the lug nuts on the camper. Andy made two trips back to the RV for tools and bug spray while I chatted with the bride. When the tire was fixed, we gave them directions to the Cosby campground and sent the grateful couple on their way. It made me feel good to have helped the honeymooners.

- *A 260-pound woman had broken her ankle somewhere on a trail. The rangers were discussing how to get her across the creek and up to the road. That event went on for most of the day.*
- *An angry woman had been beating on cars with her motorcycle helmet, cursing the ranger and other people, and putting her*

lighted cigarette into a donation box. The female ranger reported the incident, but did not follow the motorcycle people. Other rangers "headed them off at the pass" somewhere farther down the road.

- *A young man was carving names into the rocks. A park visitor had taken a picture of the guy in the act and took down his license plate number. Again, the rangers tracked the guy down.*

The park radio usually presented us with stories full of holes, often with no beginning and always with no ending. Many times we could not even figure out what was going on if we did not hear the initial report to dispatch. The rangers and dispatch did not engage in chit-chat; their exchanges were short, efficient, and sometimes cryptic, just enough to communicate clearly and get the job done. Once they had the people and equipment they needed to carry out a rescue, they didn't say much else on the radio except to report the job was done by saying "clear."

Back at the motorhome, we listened to the church group across the way in the group site singing around their campfire. It was beautiful and made me think of fairies in the forest. We complimented them on their singing and they invited us over to join them later. I didn't get it all straight on who was from where, but some were from Jamaica, some St. Martin, some Brooklyn, NY, and others from the Atlanta area. Most of them had a lovely, lilting island accent that is so pleasant to hear. Andy and I agreed that was one of the friendliest and peaceful groups of people we had ever met.

Suddenly, a piece of the puzzle was found and fit into my understanding. Not everyone was like me and had grown up with plenty of forest to wander. Twelve-year-old Kelvin, from Brooklyn, had never been in a forest. Even people who grew up near trees did not always have access to them. This was a strange and wonderful landscape for many people.

The campground had been full the previous night. On our mid-day tour, we discovered food left out and unattended at four sites and left courtesy notices. One cooler had a great big sub sitting right on top and I was sorely tempted to confiscate it. Heck, shouldn't I eat it before the bears come and get it? I figured that if we confiscated all the food left out unattended, we wouldn't have to buy groceries for three months.

We learned a new term - Bear Jam. I heard it on the radio and was sure it meant a bear was spotted along the road and all the cars stopped and people got out looking and taking pictures, creating a traffic jam in the process.

Big Creek was crazy. It was neither a holiday nor a weekend, but cars were coming into that little spot in the woods like rush hour. All the parking spaces were full, so we were trying to advise everyone to park off the road so as not to block an ambulance. I was annoyed at the folks parking in front of the No Parking signs, but they politely moved. Then, those spots were filled again in short order, as soon as we moved to the far end of the parking lot.

- *There was another bad accident the next morning involving a van full of eight Ukrainian students. We thought we heard that one had died. Traffic must be horrendous when there is an accident or a bear jam. We could hear the rangers discussing where to block off the roads and how to get the cars moving again.*

Those campground host shirts were hot. The label said 65% polyester and 35% cotton. I gained a new respect for the park rangers who wear them. They also have an additional wardrobe element: bullet-proof vests. How did they manage to look so sharp and neat when we were sweating like pigs? We changed into t-shirts for our hike. Big Creek Trail is the reason hordes of park visitors came every day. The Midnight Hole swimming hole is a mile and a half up the trail and Mouse Creek Falls is two miles up. The slope is gradual, more a road than a trail. The trail mostly follows right along the creek although sometimes the creek is way down there. It is completely wooded so we were in the shade the whole way.

Apparently, the people at the Midnight Hole were not in the park to admire the scenery or commune with nature. They were there to jump off of boulders into a deep mountain pool. Local family, church and youth groups hiked up the Big Creek Trail solely for the Midnight swimming hole. In their way though, they were getting close to nature, but not away from civilization. The steep bank from the trail down to the swimming hole has been trampled by millions of feet, and a wide swath is bare roots and dirt.

Mouse Creek Falls are on the far side flowing into Big Creek so we got a nice view, but were not close to the falls. The falls are fifty-feet high in two or three sections, depending on how much water is flowing. We spent some time watching the water, drinking some of our own, and then went back down the half mile to the Midnight Hole.

There were already dozens of people there. Some were in the water, but most were sitting on rocks and watching the teenagers and a few older folks jumping off the boulders into the creek. The young men were jumping straight down, feet first, from a good height, maybe fifteen feet. Big Creek drops eight to ten feet between two large boulders into the Midnight Hole. And it really is a hole, fifteen feet deep, surprisingly deep for a mountain creek. The forest setting is stunning with the sun shining through the trees onto the giant boulders and brilliant green water. We sat on the rocks above the crowd and watched. I noticed that people were looking at us too. I supposed we stood out in a crowd with our park radio jabbering away. I felt conspicuous, but not particularly popular or admired.

On the way down, we encountered members of a trail crew trimming the growth along the sides of the trail. A young man passed us quickly and, farther ahead, started whacking the brush with a scythe. That thing looked like a weapon from a science fiction or historical movie. When we caught up to him again, I asked about the work. There were eight sturdy young men in the crew. They trimmed about twelve miles of trail that day and alternated walking and whacking. Park rules prohibit power tools on the trails so as not to disturb the peace and quiet of the forest for park visitors.

The excitement the next day on the 10:30 round of the campground was the mad scramble for campsites. The registration board was full, but there were people waiting around for campers to leave. The occupants at two sites decided to stay another night. One woman told us she had hovered around Site 2 waiting for the people to pack up and unfriendly words were spoken. I half expected a riot to ensue. People came looking for a site all day. We sent them all to Cosby, the large campground about twelve miles and half an hour away.

Since we had to walk to check out the horse camp, we decided to walk the rest of the mile down to the ranger station to wash sheets and towels. There were nice machines there we could use, but the room smelled like something had died in it. The office was empty, nevertheless the air conditioner was set on refrigerate. I opened the back door anyway to let in some fresh air. After several weeks of gagging when I did laundry, I found the source of the stench. When park personnel set traps to catch errant bears, one of the things they use for bait is canned dog food. Someone had stowed a case of dog food in the room with the washer and dryer and one of the cans had burst open. I was arranging brochures when I discovered it on the floor next to the bookshelf. Judging from the dust, those cans had been sitting there for years. I moved them all to the dumpster in the parking lot. While waiting for the sheets to dry, I read a book about bears; how to tell a young one from a mature one (how far apart their ears are), how to determine whether they have been in the area (chew marks on trees and signs, scat, beds), how to catch them, etc. And wouldn't you know it, the bears who cause trouble in campgrounds are almost always immature males.

Ranger Taylor Kasabian was an intern ranger in his twenties or early thirties. He was burly, swarthy, and cute at the same time. His round face and cheeks were finished off with a short-cropped beard. He must have been a bit shy around us because he didn't talk much and was really soft-spoken when he did. That is not to say he was unfriendly. He always wore a smile as well. He is a hunter, fisherman, and country music fan.

Maintenance man Spence arrived in a rush with a man in a swimsuit who had run down the mountain. Another man had hurt himself up at the Midnight Hole. He slipped while climbing out of the water and onto a large boulder. He apparently broke his knee and ankle on his left leg. Spence used our radio to call dispatch and soon park rangers and an ambulance were on the way. Rangers Dennis and Taylor were preparing to hike up the two miles to bring the man out, but the injured man arrived on horseback before they hit the trail. His hero came riding up on a white horse (literally) and brought him down the mountain. He was also fortunate that there were three emergency medical technicians at the Midnight Hole when he fell. One of them had fashioned a splint with two sticks and some handkerchiefs.

Once the broken leg was gone in the ambulance, I came back to the RV but could see out the window that Dennis and Taylor were still parked up at the gate. Andy went to investigate and came back in a few minutes to say a woman had been stung by hornets and needed some Benadryl. I sent them two boxes of antihistamines and a glass of water. A few minutes later I heard sirens and went up to investigate myself. She and her husband had both been stung multiple times and had taken two antihistamines each. But her blood pressure was high; she was nauseous and she was cold. The EMTs loaded her into the ambulance and took off. Then a man came up with a teenage boy asking if anyone reported a missing kid. He had somehow fallen off the edge of the trail and slid or rolled down the steep mountain side. He was not hurt, but could not climb back up. Dennis had heard him calling and told him to follow Big Creek back down. Andy walked him back to the campground and, on the way, found a car key on the ground. It turned out to be the kid's key and it was the only one he had.

- *A large construction vehicle was chugging up a steep road at twenty miles per hour when a bear cub ran out of the woods. The driver stopped, thinking he had hit the bear, but witnesses said the cub ran under the truck, out the other side, and down the hill into the forest. They found a tuft of bear fur on the underside of the truck, but apparently there was no harm done to the bear.*

- *A fifty-some-year-old man was apparently having a heart attack at the Clingman's Dome lookout tower. He was getting worse and they decided to airlift him out. The first helicopter could not make it because of the weather. A second helicopter, we presume from another direction was sent. We did not hear anything more about it, so I could only say a little prayer that he made it to the hospital and was well taken care of.*

It started raining in earnest just about time for our evening rounds. I was surprised that ten of the twelve campsites were occupied. All the campers were huddled in their tents or under canopies to stay dry.

- *Maintenance people were doing some cleaning at a sewage treatment plant when a woman apparently had a reaction to the chemicals they were using. She was having trouble breathing. When there is an emergency, they stop all other radio traffic until it is resolved. We never heard the rest of the story.*
- *Later in the day a boy was missing. They seemed to be going on high alert when someone announced the boy had been found. They take missing person reports seriously in the park.*

In June of 1969 six-year-old Dennis Martin disappeared and was never found despite, or more likely because of, 1,400 people out looking for him. Since then, search and rescue has become much more sophisticated. They use GPS to map exactly where they have searched and where they have not. Search teams are professionally managed and well trained. Well-meaning volunteers are kept out so they don't trample possible clues.

One sunny, but still humid, day I realized there was moss on everything around us for a reason. We could start to mildew before the season was over. The higher elevations in the Smokies are a temperate rain forest. The lower elevations get an annual average of 54 inches and the higher elevations get 82 inches. That rain falls over an average of 98 days per year at the lower elevations and 127 days per year at the higher elevations. There is lush vegetation like a tropical rain forest, but with different species.

When I stopped in the ladies room, I saw a daddy long legs, a spider, a katydid, and a moth, all on the walls. Spence said I was lucky I didn't see a snake. I decided not to go in there at night.

Then he told us he once opened the women's room door and came face to face with a bear that had pushed its way in, but did not know how to open the door to get back out.

After one morning tour of the campground, we took a walk part way up the Baxter Creek Trail. A woman had asked us a few days before about the huge chimney, so we went to see it for ourselves. Maybe a quarter of a mile up, where the trail takes a sharp left, there is a well-beaten path off to the right. The first thing we encountered was stack of stones, that might have been the remains of a chimney, with a pile of metal junk on top. The metal consisted of pipes, pieces of wood stove, a coal bin, a wash tub, and other unidentifiable pieces. The park calls these artifacts. We followed the path down a hill to the level spot where a house had once stood high above the creek.

The chimney was huge and impressive. The hearth was about four or five feet above the ground. It seemed to be built of creek stones without any mortar; smaller stones were wedged in between larger ones to hold them in place. There were large quartz blocks at each end of the mantel. On the outside, a large pink stone was set in as a decorative piece. We were often asked about this chimney by hikers, but were not able to find out what the building was that the fireplace had heated. It was probably part of the logging town that used to be in Big Creek. Early park maps show the old homesteads, but they did not record the buildings in the logging town. They were all razed when the park was established. Today they would be historical, but it was not the history the park sought to preserve.

- *A fourteen-year-old boy had left the rest of his family waiting in the parking lot to walk up to Oliver's Cabin in Cade's Cove. He had been gone for several hours when the ranger called for help in searching for the boy. A short time later another ranger called from the visitor center to say the boy was there. He must have taken a different path back to the wrong parking lot.*

Two men from North Carolina State University came to the park doing virus research. They asked us if there was a place to get some electricity for their centrifuge. We offered our electrical outlet on the side of the RV and they went off to capture some chipmunks harboring the virus. Mosquitoes bite the chipmunks and then bite children who get sick. The scientists were hoping to find some chipmunks with antibodies. At the end of the day though, they had not trapped any chipmunks.

The group site had been occupied every night but one. We had a large extended family that had come every year for sixteen years. There were children of all ages from all over the place. Then came the summer-camp science kids - seven exuberant middle school kids and seven counselors. They hiked to the Midnight Hole and measured water flow. They left in their van at daybreak and hiked up Mount Cammerer. When they got back in the evening, the kids were mostly silent. On Friday, a large group of Presbyterians arrived to take their place.

Andy noted that over in the Presbyterian camp, the old people sat in their chairs without getting up. The younger folks sat in the chairs, but got up occasionally to do something. The teens sat in the chairs and got up almost immediately, and the small children never sat down. Of course, Andy sat in his chair for hours observing this phenomenon.

3

The Big Creek Park Experience

Maybe, at first glance, there is not anything special or extraordinary about Big Creek. A one-lane gravel road leads gently up a narrow mountain valley. Nothing but trees line both sides. You might marvel at how steep the mountainside is on your right or over the drop-off on your left. Then, in many places, the trees are growing right at the edge of the gravel like a natural guardrail.

One mile up Big Creek Road, you get to the parking lot and the front-country maintained area. It is well groomed and clean like a city park, thanks to Spence's endless efforts. Unlike a city park, Big Creek Campground is surrounded by forested mountainsides. Hikers, campers, and day visitors can follow several trails into a sort of wilderness. It is a populated wilderness and they are bound to meet other people on the trail. But it is real wilderness in that there is no development other than the well-beaten path itself. There are wild animals, and there is solitude in many places.

The forest around the Big Creek watershed is not dark and foreboding. The logging companies denuded the little valley of all its trees by 1920. Except for a few scattered specimens, there are no ancient, old-growth trees. This results in a sun-dappled forest filled with wildflowers in the spring and laurel, azalea, and rhododendron in the summer.

So what does this give us? Like much of the rest of the Great Smoky Mountains National Park, we have a place to get away from it all in relative safety. People get hurt in the park all the time. The ones in the front country and on the official trails are likely to be rescued. Those who strike out on their own into the real wilderness are truly on their own when they get hurt or sick. Some of them might still be out there for all we know. The rest of us, though, can wander the trails and admire the waterfalls, flowers, and views, feeling as though we are in a true wilderness while having the National Park Service at our backs. We are so fortunate to have places like the national parks to do this. We can be modern day explorers, sleep in the open, cook our meals over a campfire, and watch the stars at night.

We will have had the opportunity to search for (and maybe find) the inner peace that comes from such an experience. We can sit on a rock beside the creek and study the way the water falls over and curls beneath a boulder. There are things to think about while staring into a campfire or placing one foot in front of the other on a steep and challenging trail. Those are the private thoughts that emerge from deep inside when we have hours of undisturbed time and space for them to come to the surface.

Then, we'll get back to school and work on Monday refreshed and invigorated.

Four young horsemen were eating breakfast with yesterday's wet clothes hanging from the frames of the tent over their picnic table. Their tent had leaked and everything was wet. We wished them a drier ride today, but the rain started again just as we got back to the RV and soon it was pouring. It rained on and off all day long. The sky would be brilliant blue with small white puffy clouds, and a while later it would cloud up, get dark, and begin to rain. It was always gentle at first. Then the rain would come down in biblical proportions for maybe half an hour. The thunder would crack and rumble. Then it would clear up to sparkling sunshine again.

Ranger Tabby Cavendish is a petite red head. She was very professional in her demeanor and not as outgoing with us as Rangers Tim and Dennis. Although she appeared in Big Creek often, we did not get the opportunity to engage in much conversation with her and get to know her as well as the others. I was surprised to learn from Google that she has mapped many caves in the U.S. She is also a rock climber, static trapeze artist, and a jujitsu practitioner for exercise.

After we did our evening tour of the campground between showers, we went to the bridge in the picnic area to watch the people swimming in Big Creek. It was unbelievable that there were so many people in the picnic area with all that rain. It was more than I'd seen in the swimming hole to date. There were dozens of people having a party at the group picnic table. How did they ever keep the birthday cake dry? We saw three men catching fish with a net. They had on snorkels. Two of them would hold the net while the third slapped the water and herded the fish into it. It is illegal to fish with a net in the park, so Andy called Ranger Tabby. But, by the time she got there the men were gone.

The swimming hole served as the community pool for the locals. For them, this was more like a city park with picnic tables and a pool in which to cool off. It attracted a good number of Hispanics who were probably farm workers who needed a place to cool off and relax with their families on the weekend.

The dumpster was overloaded. There were two ears of corn, half a watermelon and several bags of garbage left on the ground in front of it. That is all favorite bear food in a campground. We found a long 2x2 piece of wood in our campsite and Andy pushed the trash farther back. It was a difficult job because the trash was so wet, the stick just poked right through it. Then we got all the stuff on the ground inside. An hour or two later, the dumpster was so loaded up again that the lid was open with trash bulging out. Another large bag of trash was on top. Tabby called to have the dumpster emptied.

The busload of kids that had marched happily to Midnight Hole as a group was straggling back in the rain, in twos and threes, with towels over their heads.

There was a steady downpour Monday morning. The thirty-somethings in the group campsite were packing up to leave. I felt sorry for them; they had steady rain for most of their visit. It was still raining when we left the park for our weekly grocery shopping. We spotted the thirty-somethings in the picnic pavilion near the power plant on the Pigeon River. At least they were not getting rained on – finally.

We bought a folding chair at Wal-Mart for Spence to sit on when he visited us during his morning coffee break or his lunch break. He got a big kick out of it, but said he had better get back to work rather than sit in it too long. His job is a bit nastier than most maintenance men. In addition to cleaning the restrooms and mowing the grass, he cleans the horse stalls when campers do not clean up after their horses, and he cleans the ashes out of the fire pits at the campsites. With the humidity, the man showed up drenched with the sweat of his labors. And yet, he had us laughing every time he stopped by. He said he is a hillbilly and grew up close to the park on the Tennessee side. He apparently had a wild and misspent youth, but changed his life when he met Sharon. He told us she had been a beautiful and feisty redhead. She spent some part of her life working as a croupier in Las Vegas before returning to Tennessee. On their first date, after they had eaten and were sitting alone talking, she asked, "Well, are you gonna kiss me or not? If you are, you'd better get to it because I like to go home and get to bed early." He kissed her. Sharon always went to bed by eight o'clock.

- ***Some missing day hikers did not return from their hike the day before. The group comprised a man of seventy, a middle-aged couple, and three children. There was a coordinated effort to have rangers, trail crew, and volunteers canvass all the trails where the group might be. The family had been overly ambitious with their planned hike and took much longer than they thought they would. They had spent the night in a backcountry shelter and were making their way along the trail when they were found. The rangers provided them with some food and water and escorted them to the trailhead.***

We spent a longer than usual amount of time visiting with the campers during our evening rounds. Everyone was so pleasant and we found ourselves chatting at each campsite. Two delightful women in Site 2 were from Asheville, NC. There were four women in Site 12, two from California and two from Raleigh, NC. They told us they had just seen a guy go past them in a kayak on the creek. Big Creek is so rocky it never occurred to me that anyone would kayak on it. An internet search turned up a number of kayaking sites that mention kayaking in Big Creek. The Asheville

Area Boating page describes it as two kayak runs, Upper Big Creek and Lower Big Creek. To paddle Upper Big Creek paddlers carry the kayak up to Walnut Bottoms, 5.4 miles up the Big Creek Trail. Upper Big Creek drops an average of 238 feet per mile, but that is only an average; there are several steeper sections. The biggest drop is about ten feet at the Midnight Hole. This is a Class V run. The take out is at the bridge in the picnic area. Lower Big Creek kayaking begins at the picnic area and runs two miles to the Pigeon River and the power plant. I found two YouTube videos of kayaking Upper Big Creek and now I know why the adrenaline junkies do it. http://dwayneparton.com/2013/12/31/upper-big-creek-another-introduction-to-creeking/.

- *A bear had made off with some picnicker's cooler. The ranger was trying to scare the bear off, but it kept coming back. Then another voice said, "Looks like we're going to have to capture this one."*

I had just started fixing our meal when Andy said he was going up to the parking lot. The meal was almost done when two boys showed up with a message: "Andy is going to be late for lunch." That meant something serious. I heard sirens. A bit later I heard more sirens. I turned off the stove and walked up to find the road filled with emergency vehicles.

A woman had slipped, fallen and apparently broken her hip. One of the trail crew men described her as an older woman and petite. That fit the description of one of the pair in Site 2. We waited a long time for the rescue squad and Tim to bring her back down the trail. When they were just about to the trailhead, her friend Barbara asked us to help her break down their campsite. Andy and I figured we would be much more helpful there than waiting to take a picture of her friend arriving in the six-wheel rescue vehicle. While we were taking down tents and packing up dishes, Barbara remarked that when I told her about the amazing variety of adventures and misadventures every day, she never imagined they would be one of them. We got her packed up, and she was ready to drive behind the ambulance to the hospital.

- *Some campers had their cooler confiscated for leaving it unattended. They were asking for it back so they could eat* *lunch. Hey, the bear doesn't give it back, why should the ranger? The rangers are nice folks and they really want to keep the park visitors safe – and happy. They may be nice, but I suspect they give the campers a lecture or a ticket along with the cooler. The fine can be $75.*

Tim and Dennis arrived just as we were making our way up to the campground on Friday morning. They came to empty the money out of the self-registration money post. Tim referred to the post as the "iron ranger." There is a registration board with pockets holding registration/pay envelopes. Campers fill out the envelope and the detachable tab. The tab clips onto the board under their campsite number and the envelope of money goes into the hollow iron post with a slot in the top.

The wonderful ladies in Site 12 were sitting around their little campfire as lively and cheerful as ever. They had taken our suggestion and driven to the Mount Sterling trailhead and hiked the two miles to the fire tower on top. It was a steep climb, up and down, but well worth it.

- *A 25-year-old woman was conscious, with blurry vision and pain, apparently with a head or neck injury. She was rappelling, lost control, and then bashed into the face of the cliff. After several hours of listening to the rescue teams figuring out how to get to the site, clearing traffic for a helicopter landing, and hiking in with their gear, the woman declined all treatment and was released.*

- *A small child had fallen into the campsite fire ring and was burned. It was not clear whether it was a big fire or a bed of coals, or whether the child had literally fallen into the fire or just tripped over the edge of the fire ring and burned hands and arms. When the ranger was talking to dispatch, we could hear the child screaming in pain. It was one of the worst things I ever heard on the radio and the memory can still bring tears to my eyes.*

Park rangers make about 100 rescues a year in the Smokies. They range from looking for lost children to carrying injured people out on a litter (a kind of stretcher). Tim said they are happy when someone turns out not to be hurt badly, even though they have mounted a search and rescue mission.

When there is an emergency, dispatch (700 is their call number) calls for radio restrictions. Only talk concerning the emergency is allowed. When it is over, 700 lifts the radio restriction and then rangers can call in driver's license and tag numbers, maintenance guys can call the shop for another part, and one campground host can call another to inquire about vacancies.

When we finished eating, we took an afternoon hike up the Big Creek Trail. We encountered a family with a dog with no leash and reminded them dogs are not allowed on the trails. The man responded, "Oh yeah, they allow firearms, but not dogs." That is the one thing people really don't want to hear. They get offended if we say dogs are not allowed on trails. One woman said, "Yeah" and kept on walking toward the trailhead as though we did not exist. You can tell him his wife is ugly and his kid is stupid, but you better not say his dog is not allowed on the trails unless you are a park ranger with a gun and a citation book.

Two women came to our site asking where they could find an electrical outlet. "Most campgrounds have one in the rest rooms." The air mattress was for Grandma who had a bad back and it was her birthday. We let them plug the pump into the outlet on the side of the RV. When they left, thanking us profusely, Andy and I agreed they had come from Site 9 where we had met Grandma earlier. Site 9 always seemed to have colorful characters in it. Later, a man arrived with a bunch of inflatable water toys looking for an outlet to blow them up with the little pump. Word must have gotten out.

- ***There was a motorcycle accident early Saturday morning. A thirty-year-old woman was in extreme pain and hurt everywhere. It was relatively soon after that the Life Star ambulance helicopter evacuation was carried out at the horse stables.***

The ladies in Site 12 questioned the toilet situation in the campground. The ladies room only has two stalls for twelve campsites. One of the toilets had been out of order for weeks. We said we would mention it to Spence. He stopped by the motorhome for a break in the early afternoon and the four women from Site 12 just happened to come hiking by. Andy invited them to discuss the women's room with Spence and sat back for some entertainment. Unfortunately, we had to listen to a lot of disgusting things that one percent of the population does in restrooms, including using the floor rather than the toilet. It was truly appalling. He also explained that he can't fix the toilet; that's the plumber's job and the one plumber for the whole park just hadn't made it over to our side of the park yet. With his animated speech, a tone of irony, and colorful language, Spence charmed them with his lecture, even given the topic.

Our mid-day meal was just about done when two fellows came off the horse trail for help. The sick-looking, red, and shaking one had been stung by hornets. He had been fly fishing above the bridge on Big Creek. He somehow brushed a tree branch and was swarmed by hornets. Then he tried to escape the hornets by getting under the water and bashed his forehead on a rock. That yielded a nice knot with a scrape on it over his left eye. I called 700 on the park radio and they called for an ambulance. The man said he was not allergic to bee stings as far as he knew, but he had been throwing up on the way back down the trail and the shaking was troublesome. I gave him two antihistamine pills and some water.

Of course, that being a weekend, the road was filled with parked cars, several of them blocking the road to our host site. Tim had radioed for one of us to stand on the road to direct the ambulance to our site, but it couldn't get past the parked cars. The man in the group site from Grace Bible Church offered one of the church vans to drive the patient up to the gate to meet the ambulance. I turned off the stove and walked up to the ambulance. Andy and I blocked traffic so the ambulance could turn around to leave.

- *I could not believe it when I heard of yet another motorcycle accident. It was the third one that day.*

Two young men and a young woman with a puppy that would one day turn into a huge black lab were heading for the trail. I told them dogs were not allowed on the trail and they never broke their stride. One of the men said in a voice surely stolen from a television sit-com, "Yes, thank you very much for that piece of information." I called Tim to see if a ranger was coming over because I really wanted that guy to get a fine. He told me that everyone was in training and he was leaving for the day. Oh well, I had to let that one go and get over it.

4

Read the Signs

The policy of the national parks is to minimize signs and keep the landscape as natural as possible. Points of interest are not marked. There are no educational signs describing the natural features such as one would find elsewhere. However, a few signs are essential.

There is a large sign at the entrance to Big Creek letting park visitors know they are in the right place. A small sign gives the distance to the ranger station, picnic area, and campground. Of course, there are trailhead signs to keep the hikers from getting lost. There is a small apparently invisible, sign at the beginning of the Big Creek trail that says no pets are allowed on the trails. The few, special people, who can see this sign don't understand English. Those who can read it think it does not apply to their dog. There are no-parking signs along the narrow roads, intended to keep the road open for emergency vehicles. You can find them behind parked cars.

The campground registration board is splattered with signs. There are large directions for registering for a campsite. Several smaller signs remind campers that they are in bear country and to keep their food, cooking utensils, and toiletries locked in their car or in the bear-proof locker. Another poster reiterates the process for registering for a campsite; set up your tent first to claim the site. Apparently, no one reads any of these.

Why? Why don't they see the signs? Why don't they read them? Why don't they obey the rules meant to keep the park safe and pleasant for all visitors? One guess of mine is that people judge the rule and, if it doesn't suit them, choose to ignore it. They willfully park in front of the no-parking sign and take their dog on the trail. Yet, I have also been in a strange place and not seen the big-as-day sign right in front of me. Some of us really just don't see the sign sometimes.

Does a normally law-abiding citizen leave civilization and come to the wilderness to escape signs and rules? Aren't the forests a place of freedom after all? Can the national parks provide us with an opportunity to be wild for a brief moment in our structured and civilized lives? This is probably something we need. We can go to a national park and be one with nature, commune with the animals, and take daring risks for the sake of adventure. Signs and rules just don't fit into that scenario.

The women in Site 12 had taken our suggestion and hiked up to the bridge up the Big Creek Trail for lunch and a swim. They loved it and reported that the water was deep there. They also reported that there must have been over a hundred people at the Midnight Hole when they passed by. That seemed likely given the situation in the parking lot. Cars were parked in every conceivable space along the road and up into the campground parking lot. There were twenty teenagers up there just from the group campsite. Well, Tim told us to give up trying to control parking and hide out at the RV if things got too frustrating. I took him at his word.

At the end of the day, Andy and I sat in our chairs and listened to the twenty teenagers from Grace Bible Church chatting and laughing. It was so pleasant to see them eating their dinner around their roaring campfire and having such a good time. We were exhausted.

- ***BOLO (Be On the Look Out) for a man in a pick-up truck. His house had burned to the ground that morning and he was seriously distraught.***
- ***A fifty-year-old woman was dehydrated and delirious at a backcountry campsite. After some time, rangers got to her with some water, but said she still needed assistance to get off the trail.***

Spence was taking a break and chatting with us after cleaning the restrooms. Three men came by on horses and were being pursued by a woman on horseback who was yelling that a horse had fallen off the trail. Spence grabbed our radio off the table and reported the incident to 700. The response was they were short on resources and it would be a while before anyone could respond. A teenage boy came down the trail and reported that the horse was OK, but they were just trying to get it back up onto the trail. A while later, another teenage boy came running to the RV to report that they needed help getting the horse out. Andy called in, but 402 (supervisory Ranger Jared) said they needed more information to know what to do. We decided to hike up to assess the situation so we could report better and were almost to the Midnight Hole when horses came walking down the trail. After much shoving and encouraging, they had given the horse some water and let it rest. When the horse calmed down, it got up and climbed the bank by itself, cut and scratched, but otherwise alright. Andy called Jared on the radio to let him know the crisis was over, but got no response. Andy tried the radio every few minutes, but no one responded. Then we realized the battery was dying. Later we learned that, as the battery is dying, you can hear but no one can hear you. We got back to the RV where the second radio was in the charger, but it still did not have enough battery power to transmit. We could hear the rangers discussing who to call and how to handle the horse situation, but could not reach them. Andy decided to walk to the horse camp and get one of the people to drive him down to the ranger station to use the radio there. But, just as he was leaving, Taylor and Jared arrived. Then the whole incident was over after nearly three hours. I was glad the whole weekend was over. Andy noted that the best thing about that crisis was that it occurred after we had finished eating.

Ranger Jared St. Clair was the supervisor for our quadrant of the park. Probably around forty with thinning hair and a handsome face. We only saw him a couple times over the years we volunteered.

On Monday morning, we decided to go check out Gatlinburg on our day off. What a tourist town. The sidewalks were packed with them. The streets were jammed with cars and trucks. It had, at some time in the past, been a beautiful mountain valley that is now filled with hotels, restaurants and various tourist attractions. We got all the way through the eight or ten traffic lights to the other end of town and the entrance to the national park. Ah, wilderness!

The visitor center was packed full of people too. We walked through the small museum which describes the various environments, plants, and animals of the Smokies. It has mounted animals, including a black bear. The gift shop was as crowded as a crowded elevator in a high-rise office building in a big city. Typical Andy and Dinata, we joined the Smoky Mountain Association and walked out with an armload of books.

A group from the Cleveland Museum of Natural History arrived at the group site in the evening. Their leader, Nathan, said they were going to stay several days and study salamanders. Andy quipped, "Maybe if they are lucky, they'll find the lizard of Oz." He knows very well that salamanders are not lizards, but will say anything to make a pun.

- *A ranger called dispatch and asked for a doctor. There had been a high-impact motor vehicle accident. The car was off the road and down an embankment. The man was not breathing. After a few minutes, the doctor said to stop all efforts. Then, there were cryptic communications among the park rangers related to controlling traffic, removing the body, and towing the car.*

- *The other radio incident, which went on most of the day, concerned a bear. The park rangers just say three-five-oh. Well, there was a 350 at a waterfall and too close to the park visitors. Three-five-one, a female voice, seemed to always get the bear herding chore. I don't know what she did to scare the bear. This bear was apparently not too scared; it kept coming back. We could hear them talking on and off most of the day about herding the bear, or tracking the bear. Later in the day 352 said, "He's walking right down the trail. I have a clear shot, but can't shoot because there are too many people in the way." They must have herded the people out of the way because 352 got him a short while later. Then we heard the announcement that 350 was in the cage.*

We had our meal on the grill when Tim and Taylor came by with a box of campground registration envelopes. They didn't stay too long as we were tending the grill, just long enough for us to tell them about our adventure in Gatlinburg. Tim told us, "Gatlinburg is the Las Vegas for 10-year olds."

A fifteen-year-old boy fell and cut his knee up at Mouse Creek Falls. It was bleeding profusely, so the dad ran down to the ranger station for help. People don't realize it is no longer an active ranger station. The closest ranger station is in Cosby, half an hour away. The dad wanted Andy to call Spence to go up the trail in the Gator to get the boy. However, Spence is not allowed to take the Gator on the trails. The boy had managed to walk down already anyway. Some park personnel just happened to be there, so they bandaged the knee and gave them directions to the hospital in Sevierville for stitches.

There was an announcement on the park radio of a severe thunderstorm warning with heavy rain and possible flooding. The prediction was for over one inch per hour. We walked around the campsites and let everyone know. Of course, the sky was as blue as could be in Big Creek at that moment.

We got back to our site and Andy built the fire. It was so peaceful sitting in the forest with a small fire and a bottle of champagne. I can't imagine much that is more tranquil. We heard the thunder, but it was far off over the mountain and we decided the storm was passing us by. I heard a soft sound. It got a bit louder. Then I asked Andy if he heard it. It sounded like rain. Then, it was rain; hard rain. We grabbed our chairs and our glasses and headed under the awning. As we sat inside and watched the downpour through the window, we could only say, "We warned them."

A friend sent an e-mail asking whether we heard about the grizzly bear killing campers at Yellowstone the day before. I was able to get on line and read about it. The Smokies only have black bears, but I was inspired to be more vigilant about food left unattended in the campground.

I decided to do a little research on black bears in the park. Bear attacks are extremely rare. Glenda Bradley was the first person to be killed by a bear in the Great Smoky Mountains National Park in 2000. There were no witnesses to the attack; her former husband was fishing in the river while she hiked on the trail. There was no evidence she had done anything to provoke the attack. In 2008, a bear attacked and mauled eight-year-old Evan Pala. The boy was saved because his father and older brother fought the bear off Evan with their bare hands, sticks, and rocks.

Because of these and other incidents, the park has made a concentrated effort to educate park visitors about bear safety. The park web site has an excellent bear page that should be mandatory reading for everyone who enters the park. http://www.nps.gov/grsm/naturescience/black-bears.htm.

5

Bears

Who doesn't love a bear? First, we love our Teddy Bear; mine was ingeniously named Teddy. What child has not been read a Winnie the Pooh story? The famous bear in my day was Br'er Fox's foil Br'er Bear from Disney's "Song of the South." There probably aren't many humans in the United States who don't know Smokey the Bear because, "Only YOU can prevent forest fires!" And, those of us over a certain age will remember the picnic-basket-thieving Yogi Bear and his sidekick Boo Boo. Panda bears became all the rage when China gave Sing Sing and Ling Ling to the National Zoo following Richard Nixon's visit to China in 1972. You could hardly see their enclosure for the crowds they attracted. Preschoolers have learned good lessons from the Berenstain Bears. And, thanks to National Geographic, we all know there is nothing cuter than polar bears frolicking in the snow. They even sell soda. Bears, I think, are why so many people come to the Great Smoky Mountain National Park - to see a real, live, wild bear.

As of 2015, we had spent a total of nine months serving as campground hosts in Big Creek. We never saw a bear there. We did see one in a tree next to the road in Cade's Cove. Traffic was backed up for a mile while everyone stopped, got out of their car, and took pictures. The bear seemed indifferent to all the commotion beneath the branches. Sure, I stopped and looked too. I have one snapshot.

We have also seen bear butts disappearing into the forest as we drove through the park. All our bear sightings were on the Tennessee side of the park where most of the people are. The bears know where the food is. Black bear attacks on humans are infrequent, but the majority of them have happened in national parks and usually near campgrounds where they have learned they can get food around humans.

According to Wikipedia, the American black bear is the most common bear species. They will eat whatever kind of food is available, and this food flexibility is probably why they are listed as "Of Least Concern" by the people who track endangered animals. There are more black bears than all other kinds of bears combined. That is in spite of the fact that they are widely hunted for food.

What we realized during those nine months of picking up food around campsites is that many park visitors have not distinguished these black bears from their cartoon counterparts. All too often, park visitors get too close while taking a photo or attempting to feed the bears. Maybe they think they can make friends with the creature. But, unfortunately, that is a death sentence for the bear. Once the bears have learned to get food from people, they lose their fear of them. Then they become aggressive and dangerous. Then, the park rangers have to put them down. I hated it when that happened and was angry with the people.

The Smokies are famous for the approximately 1,600 black bears that live there. I wonder what proportion are around the peopled areas and what proportion are in the backcountry and never see a human. Far too many cubs and yearlings are killed by motor vehicles. The interaction between humans and bears isn't the best. Too many people think bears are there to make their park experience better, but the bears didn't get that memo.

Bears are magnificent creatures and deserve to be respected because they represent nature in all its noble glory. But they're also wild creatures. Not pets. This means they're out for food. Yours if they can get it, and they know they can usually find an easy meal at a national park campsite. So when you're camping, either in a national park or somewhere else, pay attention to the rules. They keep you safe and the bears alive—two things that are important to all of us.

Two vanloads of Boy Scouts arrived about 10:00 one night. One of the leaders came and knocked on the RV because they were not sure they were in the right place. They said they would only be sleeping and then heading out early in the morning. They were from St. Louis and heading to Charleston to spend a couple of nights on the aircraft carrier Yorktown. What a wonderful adventure.

Over the years, we met many campers who were not really out there for the camping or getting back to nature. They were simply using the campground as cheap lodging on their way from one place to another. Two Texans had been visiting family in Georgia and were heading back home. Several were moving from one city to another and the campground was a convenient stop on the way. A couple were on their way to job interviews. For whatever reason they were traveling, they set up their tent, spent the night, and were back on the road early in the morning.

One of the Boy Scout leaders came over to tell us the toilet in the men's room was clogged up. Andy got on the radio to call Richard (452, Spence's team leader). Andy said, "We have a toilet jam at the Big Creek picnic area." Other voices get on the radio and say there is a bear jam or an elk jam, but Andy announces we have a toilet jam. How humiliating and, to make matters worse, he was proud of himself.

- *A man had shown a hand gun to a woman, threatened to shoot himself, and then left the car and disappeared into the woods. He had been court ordered to stay away from his wife and child the day before. He said if the police showed up, he would shoot himself in front of them. A number of rangers, as well as some county police were in pursuit to prevent a tragedy. We never heard what happened as they closed in on the man, or even if they found him. It is particularly sad to hear of someone so miserable in such a beautiful place.*

It was surprisingly cool on Saturday morning. During our morning round of the campground, Site 5 was covered with food and coolers, with no people anywhere around. We finished going to all the sites to give them a chance to return, but no one did. I never saw so much food. Site 5 had three large coolers loaded with enough for a week. A large plastic tub held other grocery items. A tote bag under the picnic table was full of chips and cookies. There were also a lot of toiletries and medicines on top of the plastic tub. Bears are attracted to anything with a scent and will check it out even if it turns out to be yucky. They also had their trash hanging on the lamp post. I never did figure out why people hang their trash bags on the lamp post hook. It is more awkward to put trash in it hanging up high rather than on the ground. Can they really believe they are keeping it out of the reach of bears? The coolers were too heavy to carry so we dragged them down the hill to the bear-proof box together. It was a struggle to get them into the bear box once we got there. Andy had to turn one cooler on end so it would fit. I emptied the food items out of the plastic bin and put them loose in the bear box. We had both worked up a sweat by the time we closed the bear-proof box. I thought we should help ourselves to some of the soda, but we didn't want to wrestle the cooler back out to get to it. "Next time." "Yeah, from now on we are going to get a cold soda for our effort." But, we never did.

Later, when the rain stopped and the sun came out, we decided to walk around again. Several campsites had been vacated, we presumed due to the rain. Site 5 was empty and we wondered whether they left because they were angry we had stowed their food for them. They sure had enough food to stay for another week. Maybe they decided to go ahead and leave since we had already carried all the heavy stuff down to the parking lot for them. They just had to get it out of the bear-proof box.

Site 3 had a lot of food out, but when I began poking around and talking to Andy ("No one is here.") a man's head popped up in the tent window and he said, "I'm here!" Oops. I hoped he was just taking a nap.

- *Another horse fell off a trail. It was apparently precipitated by hornets. The boy riding the horse was not badly injured and they were not requesting an ambulance.*

- *A man was hurt on an island in a creek. He was apparently in a difficult spot for the rescue people to get to him. They had some sort of inflatable raft they used to move him down the creek where it was easier for them to get him out.*

Spence came for a cup of ice after he had been weed-whacking along the road into the campground. He was complaining that he was whacking weeds along a ditch when a man stopped his car and beckoned Spence over some fifteen or twenty yards. "Why can't that man walk up to me to ask a question? He wants to hike a mile and a half up to the Midnight Hole, but can't walk twenty yards to ask me a question?" This was not a one-time occurrence; he said it happens all the time. Spence is really the face of the Great Smoky Mountains National Park in Big Creek. Park rangers come through occasionally, but he spends his whole day in the developed areas. People see his uniform and go to him for information and help. Park visitors refer to him as a park ranger.

49

One of the most common questions is, "Where are the bears?" One of his most common answers is, "We let them out at ten o'clock." He loves to joke, but he also loves to interact with the visitors. Every visitor who commented to us about Spence loved him.

An elderly, disabled man and two women drove into the parking lot looking for a place to park. Andy pointed out the empty handicap parking space. They asked Andy where to hike to the Midnight Hole. Andy pointed to the trailhead sign. Then one of the women asked him to describe the hole, so he did. Then they asked him to describe the waterfall, which he did. Then they asked for a description of the hike to get there. Andy said the trail is good, but one of the women was somewhat overweight and he was concerned she might not be able to hike that far up hill. The thin woman asked, "Is it the answer to a dream?" Andy replied it depends on what she dreams about. At that point, the old man started laughing so hard he began passing gas. That flustered the women, but the gas and the laughing continued. Andy just smiled. The man waited while the two women headed on up the trail. Andy never found out whether her dreams were answered or not. He was still laughing and shaking his head as he relayed the story to me that evening.

I had seen a brilliant green bug on Big Creek Trail and thought it might be an emerald ash borer, so I called the number on the bug brochure. A woman from the park returned my call about the bug. She said there are other brilliant green beetle-type bugs in the forest, so it could have been one of them. A crew of hemlock guys would be coming over and bring me some brochures to help me identify the bug if I saw another one. Campgrounds are high-risk areas for the bugs because people bring them in with their firewood. A pleasant hemlock specialist knocked on the RV some time later and chatted with us a while. In addition to the brochures, he gave me a small stack of credit-card type cards with the beetle information on it, handy for carrying in the pocket. And yes (I asked), they do know where all the hemlocks are and treat many of them for the hemlock woolly adelgid. How? Infrared mapping.

The emerald ash borer is a native of Asia. It was discovered in Michigan in 2002 and is thought to have been brought here in shipping materials. They are called emerald because that is their iridescent color. About an inch long, adults lay their eggs in the crevices between the bark. When the larvae hatch, they bore through the bark into the tree to feed, forming long tunnels. It is the larval feeding that kills the tree. They emerge the following spring by chewing D-shaped holes through the bark. Since there are no emerald ash borer eaters in the U.S., the population grows and kills nearly 100 percent of the ash trees in an area within ten years of being introduced. The infestation naturally spreads at a rate of about twelve miles per year, but spreads farther and faster by transported firewood and products containing ash bark. It has killed tens of millions of trees so far and threatens to kill all the ash trees in North America.

The Saunders clan was vacationing near Asheville, North Carolina and the three siblings, with their spouses and children, came to hike with us up the Big Creek Trail. There were twelve of us spread out on the trail, in groups of two or three, when a panicked buck with wide eyes and flaring nostrils came galloping at high speed down the trail straight toward us. No one knew where he came from or why he was running in our direction. We were all so startled that all we could do was step aside and let the panic-stricken fellow run by. When he passed most of us, he turned and ran down the bank to the creek. Unfortunately, he chose a spot with big boulders and a logjam, where he got stuck. We could see a huge gash on his chest, just above his right leg. He struggled for a while to get out of the logs and then scrambled, falling down several times, over the smaller boulders and waded across the creek. A good bit of blood from the wound washed off in the creek. Finally, the poor thing scrambled out the other side of the creek and disappeared into the woods.

- *A bear had broken into a car top and had dragged out some food. It must have been a convertible. We missed where the car was parked, but the owner was hiking in the backcountry for several days. The ranger said he could see the bear in the woods waiting for him to leave so it could get back into the car for more food. The ranger asked for a tow truck to haul the car away before the bear did more damage. Then the ranger said, "Get this: the car's license plate says, "Friend to Animals."*

Campsite 7 had a lot of food and a cooler left out. We started carrying everything to the bear box. Then the man, woman, and three young children returned in their pick-up truck. They did not know you couldn't leave food out. I realized that people just don't know what the bear regulations are, even though they are clearly posted on the registration board. People don't read the instructions or notices posted on the board. The folks who say they've been camping there for years leave their trash out. The ones who say they live in bear country leave the coolers out. Some say they put the food away at night, but thought they could leave it out during the day. Others think you put the food away during the day, but can leave it out at night when the bears are sleeping. Some probably think it is worth the risk of attracting a bear rather than lugging all that stuff back and forth. Others want to attract a bear so they get the thrill of that wildlife sighting. Then, there are those who didn't know there are bears in the park.

Two young men knocked on the door late at night. They said they had paid for their campsite early in the day, but when they came back, someone else had set up camp on the site they reserved. I explained that's not the way it works. In order to claim a campsite, you must set up your tent, and then go register. Tabby had sent them to us. The group site was empty, so we told them to set up there for the night. I didn't realize there were four of them or that they would talk half the night around their camp fire.

There were two men, a woman, and a boy in Site 12. We talked to them about bear safety and they were being quite attentive. While Andy was talking, the woman whispered to me, "We should leave the wine out so the bears will get drunk." I assured her she did not want to deal with a drunken bear, but am not convinced she believed me. Hopefully, the men had a little more sense than she did.

Ranger Dennis stopped in on his day off to run up Big Creek Trail. When he got back from his run we regaled him with our daily stories. Of course, as a park ranger he has a pack full of his own stories to tell. He always has some bit of information pertinent to our stories. When we talked of dog owners ignoring the "no dogs on trails" rule, he told us the fine could be $75 or more. We saw dogs on Big Creek trail regularly, but that was the first day Dennis saw one. However, he couldn't issue a citation wearing nothing but running shorts and sneakers.

Richard and Pat Bachor stopped in to say hello. They were the camp hosts who would replace us in September. They had been campground hosts before and shared some of their experiences with us. They did have bears in the campground once or twice when they were there the year before. He also said that a bear had stolen their sewer hose. I found that a little farfetched, but couldn't come up with another explanation for its disappearance.

- *The Balsam Creek camp host reported that a camper had not been out of his tent all day. The host investigated and found the man disoriented with slurred speech. He had "used the bathroom" in his tent. Dispatch was on the phone trying to arrange for an ambulance while a park emergency medical team went to help. Later, one of them reported the man was drunk. Stinking drunk.*

Early Friday morning a doe was standing behind the group campsite where we had seen two deer just a few days before. One of them had dug a shallow hole in the ground, but we could not figure out why.

It was nearly dark when a man came to the RV to ask about where to camp. I told him Cosby was half an hour away. Then he asked if it would be alright if they camped in the horse camp and I said he could use our phone to make a reservation. He balked at the $25 fee as opposed to the $14 fee for the regular campsites and said he would go back to the car and confer with his wife. A few minutes later his grown son came with a credit card in hand. But, when he called the reservation number, he was on hold forever. We decided something was wrong with their system and hung up. I told him to give me the $25 in cash and I would put it in the payment box up at the tent campground in the morning. We didn't know there were rules against non-horse campers using the horse camp, but no one had told us not to do that and no one else was there that night. My handling the money was also against the park rules and protocol, but I was out there in the woods with no supervision and making it up as I went.

Spence weed-whacked around our campsite and then used a blower to clean up leaves. He told us the story of when he was a hotheaded youth. Another hotheaded youth had angered him. Spence was so mad he decided to go home to get his father's gun and shoot the guy. Fortunately, his father was there to see him grab the gun. His father grabbed Spence by the neck, then lifted him off the floor and up against the wall to have a talk. This scene would have been high drama except the way Spence told it. He wasn't so much telling the story as reliving it. His hand went to his neck. His straight arms and legs twitched against the imaginary wall. Yep, Daddy sure enough saved him from a life sentence. Andy and I were howling with laughter at the scene. Later, we decided Spence missed his calling and should have been a comedian like Jeff Foxworthy. He is every bit as funny. Of course, Spence would have to say, "You might be a hillbilly...."

Spence and Tim both told us to be on the lookout for a car coming in once or twice a week. Someone had been coming in at night or early in the morning and leaving poop on the floor of the rest rooms. Spence did not specify, but Tim said it was left in the ladies room. What in the world was going through someone's mind? Andy was going to start writing down vehicle make, model, and tag number every day to see if he could identify someone coming in regularly. But the culprit was probably coming in late at night after we turned in. Andy named the miscreant of the toilet building El Excremento.

Tabby and Taylor arrived while I was fixing our meal. Andy had been checking the parking lot periodically and found them issuing a citation at the top of our drive. People were parking everywhere, as usual for a weekend. Tabby said the rangers were discussing what to do about the overcrowding. Traffic is a big part of the law enforcement ranger's job. We heard them on the radio, one after the other, all day, every day, calling in license plates and driver's licenses to dispatch, but seldom heard what the drivers did wrong.

Even though it had been raining, everyone in the campground looked mostly dry and comfortable – and cheerful. Two college-age men from Gainesville, Florida were in Site 6. They were entertaining to watch so we chatted for a while. They had their small camp stove sitting on the picnic table bench and were using small sticks to roast their hot dogs. The sticks kept catching fire and the hot dogs would drop onto the camp-stove flame. One of them would quickly turn off the stove until the dog was retrieved, the stick re-whittled, and the dog re-skewered. He told us a stick was usually good for one-and-a-half hot dogs as he was excising the still-glowing ember of the stick from the center of a dog with his pocket knife. They had been traveling for 17,000 miles around the United States and Canada visiting national parks and other natural wonders and living on hot dogs and macaroni and cheese. Their adventure story was almost as entertaining as their cooking.

You can always tell which campers have experience camping in the Smokies. The first thing they do when they set up camp is hang up a large tarp. Some hang individual tarps over the tents. There is almost always a tarp or some other cover over the picnic table and fire ring. They were ready for the deluge. Steve and Ginger in Site 10 had their old blind dog Lou with them and wouldn't be doing any hiking. They were just taking it easy under their huge tarp in the campground. The old dog put his nose up to our thighs and got to know us.

A doe was digging in the same spot behind the group campsite for about an hour the next morning. We went over to inspect after she had gone. The hole was about six inches deep and maybe a foot or so in diameter. There were roots in the hole so Andy suspected she may have been digging for them.

- *A 10-year-old boy was seriously hurt in an accident in the park in the morning. There was also a three-year-old girl who was not hurt, and grandparents were on their way to the park to get her. There were weapons in a car and someone was taken into custody. We were not glued to the radio, so we could not figure out what happened. A small child was injured and that was sad enough.*

Andy and I had taken ownership of Big Creek Campground. The park visitors were our guests. Although some were distant, most campers expressed gratitude that we were volunteers. They appreciated our advice about hikes and food storage. I figured that meant we were doing it right. Many campers also felt a sense of ownership. I can't even remember how many said, "We've been coming here for twenty (or ten, or thirty) years." They tell us how much more crowded it is now than it was five or ten years ago. I think Big Creek used to be a secret, but the secret is out, thanks to the internet.

- *A park visitor reported that a woman had given birth in a car in one of the parking lots. Dispatch wanted someone to confirm it before calling for any emergency medical people.*

- *Parents called for help when they let their children hike up a trail alone and the children did not return. The oldest was fourteen. The children did eventually make it back, late, but just fine. Dispatch suggested that the ranger counsel the parents on letting children hike alone in bear country.*

- *A ranger had made a traffic stop and the tags did not belong on the vehicle, the driver had a fake ID, and he was wanted in Florida for failure to appear in court.*

Ginger from Site 10 came to report that some people had set up camp in the woods across the creek, definitely not in the campground. Tim just happened to stop by while she was there. He said the illegal campers would be gone soon. We listened to him on the radio calling in to check on their identification before sending them on their way.

While he chatted with us, Tim said he hoped we would come again the next year. That meant we were either doing a great job or they were really desperate for campground hosts. He assured us we had done a great job. Of course, one criterion for doing a great job is being independent and not calling the rangers for every dog on the trail or every car parked along the road.

Andy started breaking camp on Sunday morning. We packed up our park radios, shirts, and keys and were ready to go when Jared and Taylor showed up in the brand new ranger pick-up truck to take us to the Cosby ranger station for a cookout. We sat in the backseat with the big guns, but they were locked up so we couldn't play with them.

The next summer, we returned to Big Creek as seasoned campground hosts for July and August.

The road in to Big Creek was in terrible condition. Spence had kept the developing pot holes filled with gravel and dirt, but he said he was told not to do that. He thought doing extra was an indication that he didn't have enough of his own work to do. He also told us he was laid off during the winter for three months. How do people manage with that much unpaid leave?

Many Park Service employees are seasonal. In 2014 the park had approximately 240 permanent employees and about eighty seasonal. "We use seasonal employees in Resource Management & Science, Resource Education, Maintenance, and Resource & Visitor Protection (Law Enforcement)," according to Dana Soehn, who had moved to the public affairs office.

Our new contact, Larry Ball, arrived to meet us and gave us some more paperwork. New tasks were to note what time the campground filled up, keep count of how many sites were filled with how many people, and get the zip code from where people brought their firewood. He gave us forms to do these and said he would come around regularly to check on us.

Larry Ball is a slender man in his sixties, with gray hair and a trim gray beard. As an ex-marine, his park uniform is always correct. He is soft-spoken, friendly, and has a great sense of humor. He loves the outdoors and, when not working, hikes the trails with his wife Kristen.

Larry is a Visitor Use Assistant, but I call him Boss Larry. In the early days of the national parks, the rangers did everything from law enforcement to fee collection. Eventually, the responsibilities were divided into several categories. The Visitor Use Assistant takes care of the administrative duties related to campgrounds, including being our point of contact.

We took a walk around the campground. It was full for the holiday weekend. All the sites were clean, with no food or coolers in sight. Except Site 12. Larry had warned us that it was a mess. There were food items and coolers all over the place. And, they had left a small Chihuahua. Larry said a coyote would likely eat him. He was definitely bear bait. Larry had already left the people a courtesy notice, but he did not move their food or dog, so we did not move them either. Some friends of Larry's were in a nearby site and I guess they were going to chase the bear or coyote away if one came. They would know if the dog was eaten because it would stop that incessant barking. It was sitting and barking on a toddler-sized camp chair tied to the lamp post. And, that is the last time I am going to mention food, coolers, and trash left out in a campsite unless there is a little more to the story. But, rest assured, it happened nearly every day and I have the muscles to prove it.

- ***Someone had reported that a man was beating a woman in a car and she was screaming "don't kill me." Rangers were looking for the car.***

It started off as a bad Saturday. Andy put his new espresso pot on the stove for his morning shot, but he forgot to put the water in it. He didn't notice until the plastic handle and the little black knob on top had melted. I was in the bunk trying to figure out why so much of the group site's smoke was coming in the window of the RV. It smelled like badly burned popcorn. It broke Andy's heart to lose his expensive coffee pot we had recently bought in a kitchen store.

When we made our morning round through the tent campground, I came across a young man next to his car in the parking lot. He was squatting next to a little backpacker's stove. I asked, "Cooking breakfast in the parking lot?" thinking he didn't want to carry the food from the car to the campsite. No. He was making himself a shot of espresso.

It was a holiday weekend, and both campgrounds were full. About nine o'clock, a few sites were vacated and new people were swarming in looking for a site. It reminded me of the land-rush stampedes the pioneers had in the old days. A couple with three children was looking for a site near the toilets, but when the wife saw Site 10 overlooking Big Creek she announced, "Heck with the toilets." They had a brand new tent still in the box and were opening it up. The woman told me it is a house. Later in the day, when we walked through again, the house was up. She said it had taken them an hour to figure it out and get it set up. It did look like a house; it even had four-pane windows.

The people in Site 12 had cleaned up their campsite and not left the little dog out as bear bait. All their food and coolers were stowed in cars. When we stopped by later, while they were cooking dinner, one of the little girls asked, "What are you going to tell us this time?" We said we were just there to say hello and thank them for putting their food away so they would not attract bears into the campground.

Boss Larry dropped in with another form to fill out. We were to keep track of our hours. The volunteer job requires 32 hours per week, but I was pretty sure we put in a whole lot more than that just by hanging around. We spent a good bit of time walking around the campgrounds, and then lingering in the parking/picnic/swimming area where people always have questions, usually about where to find the Midnight Hole. And, I figured that if we were hanging around Big Creek rather than exploring the rest of the park and environs, we were on duty.

When we made our morning campground walk, I noticed the folks in Site 1 had left some firewood and an ax handle. Spence was at the RV for his coffee break when we got back and I asked him to take his truck up to the campground so we could gather the abandoned firewood. Bless his heart; he had just poured a cup of coffee but jumped up to get the wood. He said it would not be there if we didn't get it right away.

The people in the group camp asked if elk were in the area. They had heard hooved animals go by in the middle of the night. Spence said it had to be horses; you would not hear elk. When Boss Larry arrived with the daily report, we read that three horseback riders had been reported missing in the night. They had parked their trailer in the day-use horse-trailer parking lot. They rode too far, ran out of daylight, and then could not find their way back in the dark. According to the report, they were at the ranger station at the entrance to Big Creek when they called for help. It gets really dark out there in the forest at night.

We were surprised how many campers left the next morning. We had eight vacancies out of twelve campsites at the morning vacancy report and there were still six empty sites in the afternoon. Big Creek was overrun with day visitors though. The parking lot was full and cars were parked along the roads in every spot they could squeeze into. The tables in the picnic area were all in use and dozens of people were in the creek.

We had to tell a lot of folks how to find the Midnight Hole. They drive right past the trailhead when they come into the parking lot, but once parked they can't see it. We were a lot more laid back about the madcap parking than we had been the previous year. As long as they were not blocking the road or the trail from the horse camp, they were alright. We realized we couldn't do anything about it. While we told a driver at one end of the parking lot he was blocking the road, another driver at the other end was parking in the woods. We had pretty much given up that challenge.

As would be expected, talk on the park radio was nonstop all day. There were car breakdowns, accidents, speeding, and illegal substances. There were also a number of bear jams.

The campground was practically deserted at the end of the July 4th weekend. Only three sites had tents. I was checking the registration board when Boss Larry arrived to take the money envelopes out of the iron ranger. This is no simple task. The steel is thick and heavy. He used the first key to unlock the money box from the post. He used a second key to open the money box and take out the pay envelopes. Larry said if you want to test anything to see if it is vandal proof, put it in a campground. He needed me to witness and help count the envelopes and seal up the bags with the cash and with the keys. I was dismayed someone had put a cigarette butt into the pay post. Fortunately, there were only a few burns on the envelopes and no money was lost. The park needs all the cash it can get. What was someone thinking? And, why? Are they angry with the park?

The family with the house tent in Site 10 told us they had hiked down the creek yesterday and today they were going to hike up the creek. They did not mean alongside the creek. They were literally hiking in the creek, dragging the small children over the rocks when necessary. The whole family was grinning from ear to ear. Moments like that made up for the illegal parking, trash dropping, unattended food, and bad manners.

The folks in the group site were packed and ready to leave. The man came over to thank us for Andy's help in changing his flat tire. Just as they were waving goodbye and driving up the hill, the first drops fell. Dispatch had announced severe thunderstorm warnings several times. We heard thunder, but did not see any lightning. Nevertheless, we sure did get the deluge. Cars were streaming out of the parking lot. When the first storm passed, cars were streaming back into the parking lot. We had our meal when our daughter Kathy arrived. There was another downpour while we were eating. The sides of the screen room filled with water and it was more like looking through cloudy glass than a screen.

Our daughter Kathy, the intrepid camper (or should I say the intrepid coffee drinker?) came prepared. She brought out her equipment and supplies the next morning. She had the Clever Coffee Dripper, billed as the best of both worlds: the French press and filter drip brewing. She brought a jug of spring water, an electric kettle, an electric coffee grinder, and special beans from her local coffee roasting shop. She forgot to bring the ground tarp for her tent. Andy was fascinated. I laughed, but had to admit the coffee was delicious.

We hiked up the Big Creek Trail and saw dozens of people swimming at the Midnight Hole. There must have been a busload of teens sitting on the rocks, taking a lunch break. A large bag of salty snacks sat between every two kids. Kathy and I were both overwhelmed with the aroma of Doritos in the hands of the two kids sitting on the rocks right in front of us. I considered what kind of Yogi Bear maneuver I could pull to snatch the bag and run. Usually, the people at the Midnight Hole are jumping off the rocks one after the other. This group was somewhat quiet at lunchtime. They were too busy stuffing themselves with Doritos, and probably Cheese Doodles, to talk much.

The rhododendrons along the trail were dropping their blossoms. In some places, the trail looked as though a flower girl from a wedding had made a pass through. The whole blossom-strewn trail was pink. We had Mouse Creek Falls to ourselves. It was roaring and lush after the recent rain. We crossed the upper bridge and walked down a path under the rhododendrons along the creek to some boulders. We sat there and ate our snacks of raw carrots, celery, green peppers, and cucumbers. Kathy and I talked wistfully about the Doritos.

One of the Boy Scout leaders in the group site came over the next morning and told us about an incident with their bus. It was a fancy white church bus, about the size of a school bus, but with a tractor/trailer front end. As they were driving up the one-lane gravel road into Big Creek, they encountered a car coming down. The bus stopped. There was apparently a wide spot in the road just a few yards behind the car, but the driver refused to back up. As they inched by, the bus wheels went into one of the large and growing pot holes and slid a bit into the ditch, hitting a boulder sticking out of the uphill side of the mountain. It bashed in the bus's right rear quarter panel. To make matters worse, the man in the car got out, pulled down his pants, and mooned the busload of Boy Scouts. Andy called for a ranger to come take an accident report. We laughed about the moon later.

We were part way down the campground road when we heard of an injury at the Midnight Hole on the radio. We headed to the trailhead and met Dana Soehn, the park's volunteer coordinator, who had called in the injury. She said she had come to the RV for us to call on the radio, but we were walking around the campground at the time, so she drove her car down closer to the interstate to get a cell signal. She also told me her husband, Heath, was the new ranger at Cosby. He had been working for the park for nineteen years. Ranger Heath arrived and introduced himself to Andy before heading up the trail to assess the injury. He gave Andy some paperwork for witnesses to sign. Heath was no more than fifty yards up the trail when he encountered the girl walking down. He radioed dispatch to call off the emergency. He and Andy shrugged their shoulders and shook their heads. Tim arrived just after that. The two rangers talked with the church group that included the injured girl. Tim stopped by for a visit when he was finished with the incident and told us he likes emergencies to end that way. There are enough emergencies in the park every day that do not turn out so well.

Ranger Heath Soehn is a large man, tall with broad shoulders. Even though he is in his forties with thinning sandy hair, he is still a boy at heart. A native of Gatlinburg, Tennessee, he has that soft-spoken east Tennessee drawl and a broad smile to match. We heard him participating in search and rescue missions on the park radio so often that we began to call him Rescue Ranger Heath. You are seldom going to meet a man who loves and enjoys his work as much as Heath. Many times, we saw him interacting with small children, including flashing his ranger truck lights and talking to them with the megaphone.

Two women in Site 6 were from California and were concerned about the bears. They were shocked there is not a bear-proof box at every campsite. We told them the black bears in the east, unlike their cousins out west, have not learned to break into cars yet. So, people can safely store their food in their cars. I should clarify; the bears haven't learned to break into a car with all the windows closed completely. Search for the YouTube video "black bear breaks into car in the Great Smoky Mountains National Park."

The woman in Site 10 wanted to know what people had to do to get the toilets fixed in the ladies room. It had been broken since last year when she was there. I didn't know the answer. She said she was sending in a comment card to the park about it. I decided to ask Boss Larry for some more comment cards, to give one to all the women.

- *Hikers called the park on their cell phone to say they knew where they were (atop Mount Sterling, six miles up the trail), but did not have food or water and would run out of daylight before they could make it back to Big Creek. Tim took care of it. I would tell them to sleep in the woods and hike down in the morning. Tim is a lot nicer than I am.*
- *A hiker at the fire tower on top of Mount Cammerer had fallen and apparently broken his arm. That party was just reporting*

in and said they would stay there for the night and hike to Cosby in the morning.

We were bolted awake at three a.m. by powerful thunder. The sound was similar to the cloud-to-cloud rumbling you hear in distance in the summer. But it didn't rumble so much; each clash of thunder seemed to hang in there like the bang of a gong. They echoed off the mountainsides and filled the little valley formed by Mount Sterling to the southeast and Mount Cammerer to the northwest. It was a powerfully beautiful sound.

Andy built a huge campfire in the evening. We sat out for hours watching the wood burn down to a bed of coals. There is something mystical about sitting by a fire in the dark forest. Of course, there is the comfort from the heat. But, there is also the beauty of the ever-changing flames and glowing coals and the crackles and pops from the wood. The light was flickering on the trees and leaves surrounding our campsite. For us, it was a time of quiet talk or long, comfortable periods of silent reflection. We would peacefully sit and poke at the fire with our sticks to rearrange the logs as they burned down and then watch the shimmer of the glowing coals.

The teacher from Site 3 stopped by our site to say that three Israeli men had come in and set up their tent and said they were heading out for an overly ambitious hike. He was worried they would not make it back before dark. We said we would check on them and report them if they did not get back.

- *A ranger reported a young man walking through the park with a huge cross on wheels. I imagined it was like the ones we saw pilgrims carrying (in the manner of Jesus) on the trail to Santiago De Campostelo in Spain. The wheel is at the base and they carry the cross over their shoulder. He was familiar to the park rangers. The dispatcher said someone had recently seen the guy at Wal-Mart. The ranger stopped to talk to him and reminded him to stay off the winding mountain road. The guy said he was carrying the cross over the mountains to Cherokee. Later in the day, another ranger came on duty and reported a cross-carrying man to dispatch. The concern was that a speeding park visitor might hit him and turn his cross into splinters. Of course, we never heard any more of him. He could not have made it to Cherokee in one day, so he slept on the roadside somewhere. I imagine a pilgrimage could be quite spiritual, but Wal-Mart?*

There was one Israeli in Site 10. The other two had gone out to buy ice for the cooler. His English was poor, but we struggled to chat for a while as he was preparing dinner. He asked me if I knew of a Chabad house nearby. I had no idea what one was, but Wikipedia did. It is an orthodox Judaism center that serves as a community center. The rabbi and his wife host programs, activities, and services for the local Jewish community and travelers. They are all over the world. I found one in Knoxville and one in Asheville and took the addresses and phone numbers back up to the campground. When I got there, the other two young men were dumping ice into the cooler. One of them was astounded. How did I know? When I said the internet, he was even more astounded. How did I get connected out here? It was too difficult to explain the signal booster with our language barrier.

One of them wanted to know where they could ride horses. For that information, I went to the man in Site 12 who had said he lived nearby. He told me there are places on the road between Cosby and Gatlinburg. I went back to the Israelis and described this by pointing to their park map. Again, they were impressed. No, it was more like stunned amazement.

They asked me if I was Jewish. No. They asked me if anyone in my family was Jewish. No. How did I know about Shabbat? I explained that our close friends Susan and Richard are Jewish and we had observed Shabbat, the Sabbath (and the Friday night blessing and meal) and Christian holidays with each other for many years. All three young men were grinning with admiration.

The Big Creek road goes past the day-use parking lot and leads to the tent campground. It is lined on both sides with a short split-rail fence that zigzags. I call it Spence's split-rail fence because he is always setting it back up when the park visitors knock it down trying to create a place to park. That fence was also a favorite photo subject for me as the rails were covered with thick green moss.

- *A visitor reported that someone had hit a bear with their car. The bear was dead when the ranger got there to investigate. The ranger called for someone to bring a pickup truck to pick up the bear.*

Tim was in the area just before dark. He walked around the campground and then stopped in briefly to say hello. He always made it a point to show his appreciation for us.

Big Creek was raging the next morning. We could hear it as soon as we opened the RV door. It must have rained hard up the mountain during the night; we didn't get that much at the campground. The normally clear mountain creek was muddy, and the water level was the highest we'd seen. After our campground walkaround, we went down to the bridge to take a look. The little waterfall below the bridge was barely there. Upstream was all white water.

I wasn't surprised to see kayaks; they are in the campground all the time. But the guys had carried them up two and a half miles to the upper bridge and kayaked down Big Creek to the lower bridge by the picnic area. One of them assured me no one was killed. They even kayaked through the Midnight Hole. I slipped up when I asked and called it the Mudnight Hole.

The people in Site 12 had just finished a dinner which included ramps and eggs. I had read about ramps but never seen or eaten any. They gave us each a small serving which I promptly dropped on the ground. They had plenty left over and kindly gave me another serving. Delicious. Maybe something like spinach texture, but with a strong and distinct onion flavor all its own. The older man assured me they had collected the ramps in the woods in North Carolina, not in the park.

According to About.com they are also called a wild leek. They are native to north America and range from South Carolina to Canada. Although they are an onion, it is their wide leaves that set them apart. They are traditionally eaten with scrambled eggs or fried potatoes and too many of them will give you a serious case of ramp breath. Yes, it is illegal to harvest ramps in the national park. The annual spring frenzy of ramps harvesting was wiping out the plots. It is illegal to harvest any plants, animals, minerals, or artifacts in a national park.

On Sunday morning we met a man in the picnic area who was wearing a white shirt, white tie, white pants, and white shoes. He said he was 85 and his daughter told him he shouldn't wear the same clothes all the time. So, he had the same outfit in seven colors. That included shoes and ties. He said white is for Sunday. That was definitely the character of the day.

A doe was in the group site again. She looked up and stared straight at me before putting her head back down to nibble on something I couldn't see behind the rock.

We had settled down to reading outside the RV in the afternoon when the day's excitement began. A young man came running down the horse trail, paused, looked at us, and came over. He asked if we had seen a guy running in red swim trunks. We had not. Then he told us a girl was suffering from hypothermia at the Midnight Hole. An Army medic, also at the Midnight Hole, attended to the girl and sent the young men down to call for help. Andy called dispatch and Tim responded to say he was on his way. We were to wait at the trailhead, get updates from people coming down the trail, and report to Tim on the radio as he drove the half hour to Big Creek. The missing young man in the red swim trunks had gone to his car and driven down to the ranger station where he could get a cell phone signal and had called 911. The first people to show up were the Emergency Medical Response team from Fines Creek, North Carolina Volunteer Fire Department.

Tim arrived and got some information from the crowd of teens at the trailhead who were in the same group as the sick girl. The guy in the red swim trunks was the reporting party, being one of the group leaders. One of our jobs was to keep the reporting party in place until the ranger showed up to get the report firsthand.

We got subsequent reports from others coming down the trail. She had complained of feeling funny. Her lips were blue. She passed out for about thirty seconds. She couldn't stand up. The medic had other bodies lie close to her to warm her up. They covered her with whatever articles of clothing and towels were available. She was feeling better.

Tim did a quick change from his bullet-proof vest to his rescue backpack and chatted with the other emergency responders before heading up the trail. An ambulance arrived followed by a truck towing a six-wheel all-terrain-vehicle ambulance on a trailer. Ranger Pete from Cataloochee responded when he heard how far away Tim was. The road was full of emergency and ranger vehicles.

Tim had called for the six-wheeler ambulance to go get the girl. He would meet them on the trail as they carried the girl down. Andy said he would stay with some of the other girls in the group at the trailhead to comfort them, just in case any of them needed a hug.

The ambulance took off up the trail. It was a while later when the girl, accompanied by a big group including Tim and the ambulance guys, came walking out. The six-wheel ambulance came out empty. The regular ambulance crew checked her out.

Then she posed for pictures with the medic who attended her up at the Midnight Hole and the whole group headed up to the campground. Andy and I were directing traffic on the road, since it was narrow along the curve with all the emergency vehicles parked there. Meanwhile, Tim and Ranger Pete talked with some of the emergency responders. It was all over when the six-wheel ambulance was driven out on the trailer. Tim complimented us on handling the incident perfectly. And, with that, we went back to the RV for the night. I could hear two owls calling to each other, one close by and the other in the distance.

6

The Park Radio

If there was one surprise about life in a national park, it would have to be the park radio. I had no idea how essential it would be and not just for us. It was the lifeline to all the various entities that make park life possible.

Before we left to take up our posts as camp volunteers, we bought a signal booster. We knew cell phone reception was spotty in Big Creek, and our cell phone was our connection to the outside world, so we thought we should make sure we had a signal.

A signal booster is a piece of electronic equipment that amplifies a weak cellular signal. It is just like the cell towers you see along the highway, but in miniature. An outside antenna is mounted on the side of the motorhome on a tall piece of PVC pipe. A long wire connects the antenna to the signal-boosting amplifier inside the motorhome. It works the same as signal amplifiers in hearing aids and electric guitar amplifiers - by boosting the electric current. Once boosted, the stronger signal is sent out from the inside antenna, which we keep near our hot spot. Unfortunately, we found out that a signal booster only works if there is a signal to boost. That's not always the case in a national park—and rightly so. Who wants to see ugly cell towers dotting the horizon?

The park radio became our substitute. We kept it turned on and with us at all times, and it didn't take us long to figure out how important it was. There was nearly constant chatter from early morning and into the evening. I don't mean chatter in a trivial sense of the word. The rangers call it traffic. Most of it was rangers calling into dispatch for traffic stops or emergency situations. Dispatch made announcements to the rangers regarding calls that had come into the park by telephone. They also gave impending-hazardous-weather reports. Maintenance personnel also communicated with each other by radio. Park volunteers used the radio to report problems they encountered or responded to calls for assistance from park visitors. We camp hosts also needed to call for help on occasion.

Listening to the park radio is how we learned what really goes on in a national park from day to day. We had never imagined, or even considered, all the traffic stops, accidents, illnesses, or crimes that are inevitable with so many park visitors. It was shocking to hear how many visitors crashed cars and motorcycles or how many of them were driving without a proper license or registration. We also listened in on park rangers performing rescue operations and were impressed by how organized and professional they are.

Most of the time, conversations included the dispatch office. Andy and I were constantly amazed by the apparent calm, cool professionalism of the people on the dispatch desk. They responded to ranger's calls for license plate and driver's license checks almost instantly, except on rare occasions when the system was down or slow. I talked with Bill Sorrel, the dispatch office supervisor, and asked him all my burning questions. He was happy to answer them for me:

The dispatch office is in a log cabin behind the park headquarters building. They call it the communications facility. The dispatchers sit at curved consoles with a park radio and four computer screens. They also have reference books and telephones.

The park employs seven dispatchers. They work ten-hour shifts with four days on and three days off. The number of them on duty at any one time varies. Three staff the office on weekends and holidays. Tuesdays, the slow day in the park, will have one. Dispatch operates from 6:00 a.m. to midnight and the surrounding counties handle the radio traffic from midnight to 6:00 a.m. When there is some emergency in progress, the park's dispatchers stay on duty until it is over - all night if necessary.

There are no set requirements for education and training for dispatchers, but the park usually hires people with communications experience such as military, emergency medical service, police, and fire departments. They undergo a one-year training period, somewhat like an apprenticeship.

The dispatch supervisor generates reports and statistics of the park incidents from the radio log. Most of the radio traffic is rangers making vehicle stops and calling dispatch to check driver's licenses and car tags. They also maintain park files of their stops, so they can determine whether the driver or passengers have previous incidents in the park that are not part of state vehicle records or even vehicle related. Next in number are the emergency medical service calls.

The dispatchers and rangers always sound so calm and controlled on the radio. I asked Bill if it is a stressful job. His one word response, "extremely," said it all. Apparently, there are some (park employees included) who believe that dispatchers just sit in an office and talk on the radio. Bill acknowledged that sometimes things are slow, but they are at their best during the stressful emergency and high - traffic periods. "That's what we're paid for," he told me, and I was reminded of baseball players. An *outfielder will sit and wait, and wait, and wait some more, but they're paid the big bucks to perform on demand.*

When an emergency occurs, the radio proves these are moments of "intense chaos" with constant interaction with rangers, calling for EMS, and hundreds of telephone calls coming into the park concerning the ongoing emergency. How do they keep so calm? They have checklists and priorities. One dispatcher will "dispatch" and the other will answer the phone calls. Perhaps a third will call for extra park personnel, the necessary emergency medical services, and tow trucks.

I then asked if the age of cell phones had changed the dynamics of the dispatch office. He said yes, they have more calls coming in from park visitors reporting happenings in the park. With cells phones, even park visitors can be another set of eyes and ears for the rangers—and that is always a good thing.

Communication is connection and the lines on which we connect are life lines. I will forever be grateful and just a little in awe of those behind-the-scenes people who keep our parks running smoothly, making it seem as though we have left our every-day world behind. We take them for granted, but now that I know what they do, I can't imagine the park functioning without them.

We had the dreaded trip to Wal-Mart on Monday. I managed to find a bag to carry my clip-board, brochures, and forms in when I walked around the campground. I had been carrying everything in my hands and developed severe finger cramps. Everything fit into the bag perfectly and the tan color matched my official uniform shirt. I told Andy, "I'm going to be a fashionable camp host tomorrow!" I have to admit that is a little pathetic. Andy took the picture of me proudly wearing my bag after we made the evening campground tour. It may look like a purse, but it's really a national park brochure bag.

A couple was having trouble getting the bear-proof dumpster open to throw away their trash. We went over to help, but Andy could not get it open either. It had been difficult to open the day before, and impossible that day. I called dispatch to report it and she said she would pass a notice to maintenance. Andy went back up later and sprayed the handle with WD-40, but that did not help. We heard maintenance-man Leonard beating on the dumpster first thing the next morning. Andy and I walked up to see what he was doing. When we got there, the dumpster was fixed. Leonard said he beat it open with a hammer and then lubricated it well. The bear-proof dumpsters are tricky to open even when they are working well. You stick your fingers into a slot and push with your fingertips on the edge of a metal plate on a stiff spring. Then you can lift the heavy lid. It's tough if you have fingernails. But I suppose the engineer who designed it didn't have fingernails. I wasn't going have any either by the time we were done using the dumpster for our trash.

We were just finishing eating when we saw a park employee carrying a spray bottle in the woods. He disappeared. A few minutes later, he reappeared with a big wad of something in his hand. I asked him what he had, but he didn't know. Then I recognized that it had, at one time, been an RV sewer hose. It was literally torn to shreds. He said a bear had done it and showed us the tooth marks on the fittings. The man told us bears like to chew on plastic. Then it dawned on me. The year before, the Bachors had told us a bear had stolen their sewer hose. He was a nice man, but I had decided he must be a little nuts. Now I know a bear will steal a sewer hose because it likes to chew on plastic and Richard Bachor is not as crazy as I had thought. The man had been spraying invasive plants with the spray bottle.

We had been getting an extraordinary number of deer visiting for a few days. I realized they always went to the same spot by the rocks in the group campsite. There was nothing growing there for them to eat so it didn't make sense. I went over to check it out after one left and found the rock salt from the Presbyterian's ice cream maker dumped on the ground. Another forest mystery solved.

Spence talked about his wife Sharon and how frustrated he got with her. Her COPD (chronic obstructive pulmonary disease) pretty much kept her home alone when Spence was working. When she began having trouble breathing, she panicked and called 911. Then she ended up in the hospital for several days. Spence thought the panic was part of her problem breathing. She never had trouble breathing when she was relaxed or sleeping. She apparently did not follow the doctor's orders or take her drugs as she should. Then she couldn't breathe and panicked. He got angry, and then felt bad about being angry. It sure is tough to be the caregiver.

We finished breakfast and headed out for our morning walkaround. The trees were still wet and the morning sun made them glisten. It was spectacular. The sunlight itself was almost palpable. The little orange touch-me-nots were glistening in the sun. The large patch of sun on the bridge and surrounding leaves at the creek was an incredible bubble of light. We watched the water flowing for a few minutes and then, as we walked back toward the parking lot, I turned and saw the famous smoky mist rising above the creek.

Some horseback riders stopped by to report that a tree had fallen across the trail about a mile past the upper bridge. Andy reported it to 700. Park employees seemed to be clearing trees from roads and trails every time it rained. A park employee or visitor calls the park to report the problem, dispatch asks about the size and position of the tree so the crews will know what equipment they will need, and then dispatch calls the road-clearing crew.

- *A large woman with a broken ankle was four miles up a trail at Mount Le Conte. The rangers were discussing preparations for hiking up to her and being prepared to stay overnight if they couldn't get her out – it was getting dark. One plan discussed was to carry her to the top of the mountain, about another mile up, and air-lift her out. They were calling for all park personnel in the area to help carry her out. That included interns, volunteers, anyone. For a long while, we could hear them looking for the woman. She was not where they thought she would be as she had been slowly working her way down the trail. Just before 9:00 one of the searchers found the woman and her partner. The decision seemed to be to carry in space blankets and other gear to make her comfortable for the night and carry her out in the morning when it would be safer for her and the rescue team. Then, at 9:40 they had a splint or bandage of some sort on the ankle which helped the woman walk better and they were making good progress getting down the mountain. That was the end of the story except for when they called 700 to report that they had the woman off the trail. The whole drama kept Andy and I glued to the radio all evening as we listened for each new development.*

The next morning Spence arrived in the electric-cart pickup with a tall ladder strapped onto the back. He spent all day power washing the restroom buildings. He does that a few times a season to keep the moss, mold, and mildew under control. He did not come back by until after he normally leaves for the day. He was soaked with sweat and was so hot he accepted ice for his Pepsi.

I was sad for Spence and his wife Sharon. Her COPD had kept her in the hospital more often than not since we had arrived on the first of the month. She had lost a lot of weight and had panic attacks when she couldn't breathe. Who wouldn't? Now she had pneumonia. This was the first time Spence said she was terminal. Spence and I talked about how hard it was for him to deal with her illness. He said he gets frustrated. Then he talked about how beautiful and sassy she used to be.

- *Someone reported that there were a thousand motorcycles heading toward Cades Cove. For a long while after that, others were reporting their location. The park is a popular destination for motorcycle riding. I was relieved we did not hear subsequent reports of motorcycle accidents, which we heard on the radio at an alarming rate. Eventually, someone reported that the motorcycles had left the park.*

Spence doubted there were actually a thousand motorcycles. Andy suggested that he could count the wheels and divide by two. Spence shook his head at the thought and Andy retorted, "Hey, you're getting this method from a PhD." At that Spence left with his coffee, still shaking his head and muttering.

When we got to the registration kiosk in the tent campground, a young woman asked us if we had any change. The campground fee is $14 and people often don't have the right mix of bills. Andy had already exchanged all his ones that week. She was only a dollar short so we told her to just pay what she had. We probably shouldn't do that, but I couldn't see her driving to the next exit on the interstate and back to get a dollar when some people don't put any money in at all.

Spence came with a leaf blower and blew the leaves off our campsite. He said that was so we could see any snakes that decide to join us. Spence does not like snakes in his campground. He said they have 800 square miles to roam around and did not need the campground.

Rescue Ranger Heath arrived with a tool for us to help people with car trouble in the parking lot. It was a combination air compressor, jump-start cables, and a 12-volt power source. He and Andy studied the instructions and tried to figure out every feature. It's a guy thing. It weighs a ton so I sure wasn't gonna be lugging it up to the parking lot.

Heath told us about the rescue of the lady with the broken ankle we had listened to on the radio. They got the woman off the trail at 12:30, and he got home at 1:00 a.m. He said it often happens that what sounds like a terrible problem when reported turns out not to be so serious after all. That woman walked out with the splint.

On the way through the parking lot Saturday morning, we saw a hiker who had been out on the trail for three days. He was terribly excited as he had been at one of the backcountry campsites when the rangers sedated a pesky bear and loaded it into a vehicle for transport to a less frequented part of the park.

There were several traffic jams in the campground parking area, from people looking for a place to park and turning around when they couldn't find one. Part way down the road, two vehicles came face to face with no room to pass due to all the cars parked on both sides. We stayed in the parking area for a while helping people find a place to squeeze in without blocking the road, or sending them to the horse-camp day parking. During a lull we went back to the RV to hide out.

Spence was spraying the sidewalk with a weak bleach solution. He said he was going to pressure wash the sidewalk the next day. The bleach was to keep the sidewalk from getting mossy and slick.

Tim was right. He told us we should take a day off and leave Big Creek for fun, rather than just the usual Monday grocery shopping and laundry. Andy did some research and chose an easy hike on the Appalachian Trail from Newfound Gap. We also visited the Mingus Mill. It was a long and relaxing day off and I was refreshed and ready to haul coolers to the bear-proof locker the next day.

I wanted to get an early start on the campground rounds the next morning, so I could get a head count for the night before. Spence was pressure washing the sidewalk and handicap parking spaces as we walked by. Site 6 had a huge blue tarp covering most of their campsite. They camped there often and were prepared for rain. The party consisted of a man, his father, and his two sons. The youngest appeared to be ten-to-twelve years old with carrot-red hair. Andy asked him what he would do if he saw a bear.

"Run!" Andy countered that a bear can run a lot faster than he can and what was plan B?

"Climb a tree." Andy told him a bear can climb a huge tree in a few seconds. Then he gave the bear lecture. Back up slowly without taking your eyes off the bear. If there is more than one person, stand close together to look bigger. Make a lot of noise. If the bear seems aggressive and approaches, throw rocks at it to make it go away. Andy was beginning his food storage lecture when the man interrupted. They had solved the food storage problem. They didn't have any food and were going out to get a fast-food biscuit for breakfast.

The campground was full by late afternoon and we had several parties looking for a campsite. A man and woman came to the RV telling us the campground was full and that we should have the authority to let them stay on one of the group site tent pads. That would be nice, but we didn't know if someone else made a reservation for the group site. We suggested they go to Cosby. Later, in the evening, a group of teens came and started to camp in the woods behind the group site. Andy told them to go down to the ranger station to call and make a reservation. We did not see them again.

The first missed photo op on Thursday was a string of horses. A man was on the first horse and there were maybe five unridden horses tied closely together before the last one with another man on it. They went by at a good clip, too fast for me to grab the camera. The second missed photo was late afternoon when they returned and all the horses in the middle were loaded with camping gear for the trail crew. The trail crew had been out on the mountaintop all week. They walked down in the afternoon.

- *A woman with a broken hip was about half a mile up a trail. Rescue Ranger Heath was on the case. We listened as the drama unfolded. When an incident is reported, an available ranger is assigned to be In Charge (IC). They talk on the radio with dispatch as others say they are available, or they ask dispatch to call a ranger from home. They make a call for people to help carry the litter to get the person out. Dispatch makes the calls for an ambulance or wrecker, or both. Most of this happens while the rangers are enroute to the patient. When someone gets to the patient, they report any updated information to dispatch and the others. Things often change as the situation develops. That night, some helpers on the way up the trail were delayed by bears on the path.*

Spence had been buckling down to get Big Creek ready before his two-week vacation. He had been weed whacking, mowing, and cleaning ashes out of fire rings. I've never seen anyone work so hard. Larry says Spence sure goes to a lot of trouble to make us think he's working.

There were four vacant campsites in the morning. Someone had filled out a pay envelope and put the stub underneath the stub for site four. The guys in Site 4 were a bit upset because they had not planned to leave. One of them came down to ask us if they had to vacate their site because someone else paid for it today before they did. No. This really is one of those places where possession is nine tenths of the law. There was a stub on the board for Site 11, but no one was in the site. We pulled both the stubs. This is a first-come, first-served campground, but people try to reserve one by putting a stub up early. The instructions clearly say occupy the site, set up your tent, and then go register. The instructions are written in large print on the registration board. Doesn't anyone read anything anymore?

Some campers had left their dog in their van. The young pit bull had managed to push the rear window open and get out. The people in Site 8 had captured him. Larry asked if we had rope (of course Andy did) and went back to the campground to get the dog. I started cleaning up the lunch dishes while he was gone. I had already scraped the steak bits into the trash can, but dug through it and pulled them back out again. I put the bits of meat and fat into a paper bowl. When I came out of the RV with the smell of steak on my hands the dog fell in love with me. He gobbled up the scraps in about 10 seconds and then drank from the bowl of water I set out. Whenever I was out of the RV, the dog had his eyes on me. I know love when I see it. He was not there too long before the owner drove up to retrieve him. The dog, Brendan, did not want to leave. He lay down and the guy had to drag him back to the van. The man said he was a rescue dog, and they were trying to find a home for him. He would have happily left the dog with us. Sweet as he was, I didn't want a dog that big, especially in a small motorhome.

Spence came by for his morning coffee and brought us new, permanent name badges with the national park insignia from Larry. I really felt official and proud of my new name badge. When we made our morning rounds, one of the guys in Site 4 pointed out that my badge was on upside down. Well, it didn't come with instructions.

Andy spent most of the day in the parking lot and campground. He started off trying to ease the weekend traffic situation by sending people to the horse camp day-parking area. In the midst of this he heard some guy telling his friend he had put his keys and wallet in the back pocket of his bathing suit and jumped into the Midnight Hole and lost them. They were trying to decide what to do. Andy told them he could use the radio to call for help and called dispatch. The driver of the vehicle and another friend decided to run up to the Midnight Hole to look for the keys. The driver of the second car in the group closed his trunk and then realized he had locked his keys inside. Now Andy had two lockouts. While they were gone, the wrecker arrived with a kit to unlock the car. He opened up the car with the keys in the trunk and the driver paid him $45. The woman from the first car paid him $45 to open up their car, but they still had no key to drive it. Andy suggested to them that the other car, now operable, drive down the hill to get a phone signal and call the rental car company for the first car. The company said they would pick up the people and give them another car. Andy told both of them that in five years this would be a funny story. One of the daughters retorted, "Maybe longer than five years."

- *At 3:30 we heard a call to 700 to report a drowning at The Sinks. A female juvenile had fallen into the water and disappeared. She had been down about eight minutes. I bit my lip. Rangers, divers, swift-water rescuers, ambulances, and volunteers were on the way immediately. Andy and I hung by the radio. She was twenty minutes in the water when help arrived. She had apparently been stuck in rocks and held under the water. My stomach was churning listening to the rescuers talk. At thirty minutes, we realized she was still in the water. I started to cry; it was so awful to listen. Volunteers had closed off the road. The rescuers had arrived. Later, someone asked 700 to send a minister. Dispatch already had several standing by, waiting to be called to the scene. Still later, someone called for 700 to arrange for some big flood lights to light the scene after dark. They were expecting to be there for a while. That must have meant she was still in the water. We learned she was eleven years old. I cried again for her parents and prayed they wouldn't be tortured with guilt for the rest of their lives.*

We left the RV for our morning walk around the campground and encountered a Boy Scout leader and his Boy Scout son from the group site walking down the road. The father had a dive tank on his back. I asked where he had been diving and he said the Midnight Hole. Andy and I asked in unison if he had found a wallet and some car keys. He had! He was quite surprised that we guessed. We told him they had just been lost the day before.

Why had the scout leader brought a dive tank? The year before, they had snorkeled in the Midnight Hole and found sunglasses and decided to bring a tank to see what else might be at the bottom. We were wondering how to return the wallet and keys to the German tourist without mailing them back to Germany. The man needed his wallet here. Then Andy said the SUV might still be parked in the lot. Maybe we could leave a note on it or something. The four of us walked up to the parking lot. The SUV was still there – and the door was open. Two men were behind a vehicle in the next parking space. One was the German man and the other was a locksmith who had just finished making him a new key. The Boy Scout leader, who knew the German's name from his driver's license, called out.

"Hello Herr Fischer!" The man looked up in stunned surprise. Then the Scout produced the wallet and keys to the amazement of the German and the locksmith. We continued on up the road to the campground marveling how things worked out. If we had left the motorhome a minute later, we would not have passed the Scouts on the road. They would have gone back to their campsite and mailed the wallet back to Germany. We all got to the SUV just as the locksmith was finishing up. Another minute or two and they both would have driven off. It all worked out in a marvelous series of coincidences.

Spence had arrived for his morning coffee and we were chatting, when we heard a maintenance person report a drowning at Metcalf Bottoms. The three of us gasped and moaned in unison. I don't think I could bear two drownings in two days. Fortunately, the eleven-year-old boy did not die. They got him out of the water. He was having trouble breathing, but he <u>was</u> breathing. Rescue workers were on the scene within minutes.

While the clothes were washing and drying at the ranger station, I took a three-ring notebook in the desk, went outside, laid it on the sidewalk, and took pictures of the contents. It contained a short "History of Big Creek" and some old photographs, which are posted on my blog site, Big Creek Journal. According to the paper and a little bit of Google searching, Revolutionary War soldier, Colonel Robert Love (1760-1845), owned a huge swath of western North Carolina. He had surveyed the line establishing the border between North Carolina and Tennessee and was also the founder of Waynesville, NC. The first known settler in Big Creek was John Bettis, who bought a parcel of land from the Love family in 1862. There were never many settlers living in the Big Creek area due to the lack of flat, arable land. Logging operations began in the 1880s and six logging companies operated there over the years, stripping the mountains of their trees. The last company, Suncrest Lumber, cut spruce for the war effort between 1917 and 18. The Civilian Conservation Corps moved into the group and host campsite area of Big Creek in May of 1933. They turned the ravaged land into the beginnings of a national park in Big Creek, by improving the road and building trails, and by constructing campgrounds, toilet buildings and the ranger station. I assume they were also responsible for demolition of the logging operation and the accompanying town of Crestmont. The forest in Big Creek is littered with bits and pieces of the logging mill and town.

Boss Larry sent us the Weekly Incident Report including the eleven-year-old girl's drowning and a picture of the rescue operation. On a happier note, the report also included an incident involving rangers from Cosby:

"Cavendish (Tabby), Kasabian (Taylor), and St. Clair (Jared) investigated a report of a dying hog just off the road in Greenbrier. Cavendish, excited to finish the job, was sad to find the hog to already be deceased. The hog had apparently succumbed to some sort of disease, as it was covered in a yellow funk. Kasabian heroically moved the hog out of the public eye. St. Clair supervised.

"During the aforementioned hog incident (see above), Kasabian was ambushed by several bees, getting stung on the arm. St. Clair was also approached by a bee, except he was able to use baseball skills to "hit one out of the park." Cavendish supervised."

We also learned where Tim was going; "CONGRAT-ULATIONS to Tim Rand for his new job at Delaware Water Gap!"

- *Two park men had been talking most of the day. They saw smoke in the park and were trying to find the fire. They were moving to different positions to get a fix on it. They were still talking about it in the evening. One said the smoke was white and there was no black smoke, but I could not interpret that.*

- *Another young bear was apparently hit by a car. A park volunteer calling 700 asked if he should move the bear out of the road. When 700 asked how much the bear weighed (they get up to three or four hundred pounds), he answered "50 to 75 pounds." People drive too fast on the park roads and young bears are not car savvy.*

- *Two rangers headed to a campground to investigate a domestic violence incident. When 700 checked the records, the male had a history of violence, with several restraining orders in place, and was considered armed and dangerous. A few minutes later the incident was resolved with a verbal warning and campground neighbors were instructed to report any more problems.*

I had the pot in one hand and the spoon in the other, ready to spoon the rice onto the plates for dinner while Andy was putting the silverware on the table and drooling, when a fellow came up and said his friend had dislocated his ankle on the trail. Andy called 700 and Tabby responded saying she was on her way. She asked the guy's weight, which was 250 pounds. She asked if he could walk. Andy relayed that he was slowly hobbling down the trail.

Andy and the reporting party walked up the trail until they met the injured man about three-quarters of a mile up. He was with a woman and another man. The three of them were Spaniards. Andy asked about his condition and the man said he would continue to walk. He told Andy he was having trouble walking because he had a lot of pounds. Andy replied he had a similar problem; he had a lot of years. As he walked he seemed to feel a little better. Tabby called asking for updated information. Andy reported that the injured man was doing better and would make it down to the trailhead. She said she would show up at the trailhead and decide what to do from there. When she got to the trailhead, Andy reported that the man was doing fine and didn't want any medical help. Tabby said she would go about her other business and return if she was needed. I was walking up to the trailhead at that moment and saw Tabby speed away, surely relieved she did not have to haul out a man twice her size. Andy regaled the group with his corny jokes and kept them laughing all the way down to the trailhead. The whole party shook Andy's hand before they loaded the injured man into the car.

There was smoke in the air on the campground road Saturday morning, coming from all the campfires. The smell of bacon was hanging in the air too. The morning sun was shining through the trees and the smoke, creating a beautiful scene that smelled good.

I saw the Baxter Creek trailhead sign several times a day. In addition to the standard wooden trailhead sign with white lettering, there is a small green metal plaque tacked to the post with a white diamond and an arrow pointing across the bridge. It says, "Benton MacKaye Trail." One day I looked closer and wondered who Benton MacKaye was. What did he do to get a trail named after him? I asked Wikipedia and learned that Benton MacKaye was the father of the Appalachian Trail. As a co-founder of the Wilderness Society, he presented the idea in an article in 1921 titled *An Appalachian Trail: A Project in Regional Planning*. That was a man with a vision.

Spence dropped in for his cup of coffee after he had cleaned the restroom in the picnic area. His wife Sharon was home, but had been in the hospital most of the week.

A woman with a small boy came knocking at our door. The little boy's finger tips were all red. He had screamed with pain and she thought he had touched the camp lamp, which he denied. The mother wanted to know if millipedes had caused the problem. Did I know anything about millipedes? Well, no. But Google did. The Bug Guide said they are non-toxic, but some discolor the skin. Another paragraph said some secrete cyanide and not to allow children to pick them up. Too late for that advice. The picture looked like the millipedes we saw in Big Creek. A long body covered with dark brown or black plates trimmed with bright yellow. So the color came from his playing with the millipedes. But there seemed to be blisters on some of his fingers. He no longer denied touching the lantern, but wouldn't admit to it either. I guess he learned a lesson, but I don't know what it was.

The next morning a shiny, solid brown millipede was walking down the sidewalk by the toilet building. I put my camera to the ground and took a picture. After I got the picture on the computer I could see all those legs. I clearly did not know the difference between centipedes and millipedes. I did some Google Image searches and found a simple explanation. Millipedes usually have two pairs of legs per body segment while centipedes usually have one pair per body segment.

- *A park volunteer called 700 to report that a park visitor had fallen off the overlook at Newfound Gap and was at least 150 feet down. The volunteer could hear the man calling for help. Immediately, the rangers were talking to each other, stating their locations and that they were heading in that direction. They were coordinating who was going to bring Rescue One. They were looking for rope-qualified rangers to head up there. Several people at the site made it down to where the man had fallen. Eventually, the man walked out on his own, though bumped and bruised.*

- *At the same time, another person called in from the Primitive Baptist Church in Cades Cove to report a man having a heart attack. Blood was coming out of his mouth, he was going in and out of consciousness. The man was talking a little bit, but was hard to understand. The last I heard of the incident was that they would take him out with an ambulance rather than a helicopter.*

It was a quiet day for us. We did not find any food left unattended in the campground. We chatted with people and answered the camper's questions. The day people coming in to the Midnight Hole had plenty of parking. It was quiet at the swimming hole all day. School had started and it was a relatively cool day. That explained it.

Spence returned from vacation on Saturday. He had spent most of the two weeks in the hospital with Sharon who was back home. He said Hospice would start coming to the house on Monday. They had come once before, but Sharon got better and they stopped coming. He hoped they could keep her on her medication and breathing easier. It had to be better than calling for an ambulance and going to the emergency room within a day or two of returning home.

In the midafternoon a teenage boy drove up and asked if this was where to get first aid. His younger brother had fallen at the Midnight Hole and had a bad cut on his hand. I told him I had some first aid supplies. He was a bit panicked and asked if he should take them or bring the boy here. He had run and the rest of the family was still on the way down the trail. I said, "I'm a mother. Bring him here and I'll bandage the wound to stop the bleeding until you get him to the emergency room for stitches."

While waiting for the patient, I finished washing the dishes and got out my case of bandages, tape, and some hydrogen peroxide. The patient arrived fifteen or twenty minutes later with his parents and three teens. The chubby ten-year-old was clearly traumatized. I told him to hold his hand under the faucet and let the water wash the wound. His mom held his hand the whole time. Then I poured the hydrogen peroxide over it. I have to admit I winced when his mother moved her hand to expose the wound. The deep cut went from the base of his little finger all the way down the side of his pudgy palm. His mother held the cut mostly closed while I wrapped it. Then we had him lean over the sink and washed the blood from his bloody nose off his face. Andy whispered in the boy's ear that this would be a good time to ask for some ice cream. Maybe he did after he got the stitches in.

It had been a cool night and Sunday morning was clear, dry, and beautiful. For some reason, 700 could not understand me reporting the vacancies on the morning vacancy report. My voice was "digitized." That means I sounded like a computer-generated voice with a lisp and a stutter. We heard it happen occasionally with other park personnel. Later in the afternoon 700 reported that the Mount Sterling repeater was not working. No wonder the radio was so quiet all day.

Spence told us that Sharon was in the Critical Care Unit. We didn't know if that was the end or whether she would go back home for Hospice Care. Spence had not seen the doctor since she was admitted in the night.

Dispatch announced that the National Weather Service was warning of severe thunderstorms and heavy rain with a lot of lightning. We could hear the thunder in the distance, and eventually we got a good rain shower. Andy built a campfire when the rain stopped, and we sat outside watching the fire with water dripping on us from the trees. There was no one in the group site, so we had peace, quiet, and isolation. The freshly-washed forest smelled wonderful, mixed in with the wood smoke. The frogs and bugs were drowning out the sound of Big Creek down the hill. The warmth from the fire felt wonderful contrasted with the delightful cool drips of rain from the trees.

Tuesday was a sightseeing day, and we went to Cataloochee Valley, just sixteen miles across the mountain from us. It was early evening before we got back to our campsite. We had just set up our computers when we heard a voice outside. A man came up with a hound dog that had followed him "at least eight miles" on the trail. The dog was limping. The man said the dog was drinking from the streams and he had fed him a granola bar. He was a large beautiful hunting dog. I fell in love right away and wanted to keep him, but I called 700 to report the found dog. He said he would leave a message for the morning dispatcher to get in touch with someone to come pick him up. Andy hoisted the dog into the RV, and he lay on the spot where we dragged him just inside the door. The dog would not even stand up until the next day.

That was a serious hunting dog. He had a Garmin GPS collar with two antennae. Or, is that antennas when it is not on a bug? The poor dog was exhausted. I found a few slices of leftover turkey, some pepperoni slices, and a cheese stick to feed him for supper. He took them gently from my hand. The dog slept soundly in the RV all night. We left a light on so Andy could see the dog and not step on him when he got up in the night. The next morning, Andy took him out for a short walk up to the parking lot and back. The dog never got up again after that. We didn't have any dog food on board so Andy gave the dog a slice of bread and scrambled him two eggs for breakfast. He seemed happy. Andy found a label on the dog's collar with a man's name and phone numbers. I called 700 on the radio and gave him the information. He called back a short time later to say someone would come and pick up the dog before noon.

Spence arrived late for his morning coffee. He had extra duties in Cosby while Richard was off for the week. Sharon was still in the hospital and not doing well.

Boss Larry arrived and we chatted for a bit before the dog owners arrived. The dog did not seem to pay too much attention to them when they arrived. They said the dog had gone over the ridge yesterday and they lost track of him. They were training him to hunt bear.

Andy had been thinking about it and asked Tim if a stun gun would work on a bear. Tim did not think it would have any effect and explained how his works. He showed us a cartridge that looks pretty much like a small cube-shaped printer cartridge. He said the inside has two fish hooks on wire. When he shoots it (up to about 25 feet) the fish hooks shoot out and grab onto the person. Then, when he squeezes the trigger, they get an electric shock. He demonstrated by squeezing the trigger and we could see the current arc. He can also just press the gun against someone, a leg for instance. If the fish hooks just grab onto the bear's fur, it would not get much of a shock. He said that is true of people in loose or thick clothing too. So, we can forget using a stun gun as a means of bear protection.

We had more sad, serious conversation about Sharon. Spence was convinced she was going to die soon. He said he was angry with her for dying. I assured him that's only natural. He did make me laugh out loud and long. He admitted he has a temper and it does him no good. He told us he is not as bad as he used to be when he was younger. "I would have marched into Hell with gasoline pants on."

Boss Larry showed up with a birthday present for Andy. It was a six-inch-tall troll made of natural materials gathered from the forest. He came with a leaflet describing all the troll characters the workshop makes. This troll is the Trail Guide Troll; an acorn cap in his hand has a compass rose in it. I had to take some pictures of him to document the gift and decided he would look best in his natural habitat. I set him on the moss, among the poison ivy, and up against a tree and took his picture. I especially liked his nuts-n-seeds hat. Andy wanted a picture of the troll sitting on top of the hat on Andy's head. He said to caption the picture as: "Now, where is that troll?" When we finished playing with him, Andy set him up on the dash where we mount the GPS. That seemed appropriate for a Trail Guide Troll. Check them out at http://www.trolls.com.

When we walked up to the campground Wednesday morning, Spence was in the parking lot talking to two other park employees who were there to fix the broken toilet in the men's room. Spence called me over and gave me two fancy walking sticks. He said he got one for Andy for his birthday and decided to get me one too. His sister and her two sons make them and sell them in Cosby. Then he assured me they were the cheap models so I wouldn't protest too much. It was such a nice gift; all our previous walking sticks had been picked up in the forest. These two had the bark trimmed off in spirals and were finished with varnish.

When Spence came for his coffee, the birthday cake was still warm and the three of us had a slice. Then, when Spence was ready to get back to work, I wrapped up a piece of the cake for him to take home to Sharon.

Heath stopped by in the evening for a piece of birthday cake. He, Taylor, and Tabby had been out in the woods all day checking patches of ginseng and marking the plants with paint so they could be identified as coming from the park. This way, they hope to discourage poachers. It is illegal to harvest any plants in a national park. I sent three pieces of cake with Heath for Taylor, Tabby, and Tim. Heath told me not to ask Tim whether he got his.

- **A dead horse was on the trail near one of the back country campsites. It did not have a saddle on it. Andy commented that we could sit there all day and listen to the radio and write a book. So I did.**

We stood on the bridge at the swimming hole and watched the water pass below. Just downstream, I could see signs of fall. A large swirl of orange and yellow leaves was floating on the surface of the water in a calm corner.

A hiking club was in the group site for the weekend. They stay in a different campground and hike different trails most weekends. One of their members brought a huge ice cream maker, but their inverter did not have enough power to run the motor. They brought the machine over to our site and asked if they could plug in to our RV. Home-made ice cream? Heck yeah. When it was done, Andy and I got the first servings.

We ate leftovers for dinner and then took another walk around the campground. I saw an elderly woman with a cane walking up the path along the creek and went down to meet her. She told me she was almost 98. I told her she was my new hero. She said she would not be out there if her daughter-in-law had not brought her. She pointed out two women walking on the rocks in Big Creek and said they were her granddaughters.

We went up to the campground to see Ginger and Steve from Cincinnati. Their friends from Nashville were there with them. We had met them the previous year and were so happy they made an effort to get there before we left so we could get in a good (if short) visit. Andy invited them to our cookout. Daughter Jennifer and son-in-love George arrived from Wisconsin and we invited Tim, his wife Kendra and baby daughter Becky, to meet Jennifer and George. There were ten of us plus Becky, so we moved over to the vacant group campsite with three picnic tables and huge mega-grill.

After dinner, we moved back to our campsite for a campfire. Heath drove in to crash the party with his ranger-car lights flashing. Then we learned a secret. Policemen go for doughnuts and coffee, but park rangers go gaga for marshmallows. Actually, all of us loved the S'mores with the premium dark chocolate bars Andy picked out at the grocery store. Tim and Heath transformed into 8-year olds. S'mores and plain marshmallows did it. Those big professional law-enforcement rangers toasting marshmallows are something the rest of us still talk and laugh about. Heath told me later that we were the first campers in his career who actually offered him the campfire delicacy.

Spence came for coffee early on Wednesday morning. He regaled George and Jennifer with his hillbilly stories. Spence went to work and we took one last walk around the campground. We gave our last campground vacancy report. We stopped to visit with Ginger, Steve, Yavi, and Randy in Site 12, and then followed the path along the creek to the bridge. We left Big Creek in the afternoon and thus ended another season.

7

Park Visitors

We love our national parks. According to the National Park Service, over 305 million people visited them in 2015. I bet there were a few more they didn't count. Even those who do not visit a national park love them. We are proud that our nation has preserved these wild places and the plants and animals in them. In our fast-paced modern, high-tech world, few of us have easy access to wilderness. The U.S. Census estimates that 81 percent of us live in urban and suburban areas.

In our little microcosm of the park system in Big Creek, we met people from all over the United States and a good many from other countries around the world. They were young and old, families and singles, rich and poor, sophisticated and not so, highly educated and somewhat lesser so. Most were pleasant and friendly, many delightfully so. A very few were sullen, angry, or downright rude.

People who love the outdoors generally try to take care of it by keeping their campsite neat and clean. They did not leave food unattended. When they left, the campsite showed no sign they had been there. Others were not so careful and left food and garbage in their campsite. Some left trash in the fire ring when they decamped. A few threw food waste into the woods. Hey, it's biodegradable, right? They obviously weren't thinking about attracting bears into the campground.

Part of our job as camp volunteers was to survey the campground and the campsites. It was actually fun. Some campers set up camp with one of everything sold in Cabela's, including the kitchen sink. Others had nothing but a hammock strung between two trees. The regulars brought huge tarps to cover as much of their campsite as possible. Others got wet in the almost daily downpour. We saw two young men grilling steaks that covered the whole grill. Two others roasted hotdogs on what looked like chopsticks over a small camp stove. Campers dragged huge coolers and plastic totes filled with food and drink from the parking lot to their campsites. I'm sure some of them brought enough food to last a month if they somehow got stranded in the wilderness. A few memorable campers brought enough beer to keep themselves snockered for the whole fourteen-day camping limit. The day visitors in the picnic area often left trash in the grill.

Not all of it was intentional. The parking lot was regularly littered with small items dropped while unloading and reloading the car. We found enough t-shirts, socks, swimsuits, and flip flops to open a boutique. For some reason, beer and soda cans were often set on the ground in front of the vehicle and left there. After picking up dozens of them, I decided that was maybe the most rude covert littering a person could do.

People came to Big Creek for many reasons. The most obvious reason is to escape modern life and enjoy sleeping in a tent in the forest and cooking meals over a campfire. Others camped one night as a staging area for a long backpacking trip in the backcountry. Some lounged around the campground and creek the whole time while others hiked all day and returned for supper.

Campers came for spring wildflowers and fall foliage. We saw family and church reunions, long-distance friends and siblings meet at Big Creek to spend quality time together. A number of them meet every year. One camper we met came out to get some exercise hoping to lessen the effects of Parkinson's Disease. Some campers are really travelers who use the campground as overnight lodging during a long journey.

Apparently, all of them come to build a campfire and satisfy that deeply imbedded need for the fire's warmth and protection, and its ability to give us the space to meditate.

Day visitors also come for a variety of reasons, some the same as the campers. Researchers ranging from elementary school children to university professors came to study the plants and animals. The picnic area and small swimming hole next to a footbridge over Big Creek are a big draw for locals, especially on summer weekends. The vast majority of day visitors come to Big Creek for the Midnight Hole. They come from Asia, from Europe, really from all over the world. The locals come by the busload from Knoxville, TN and Asheville, NC and all the small towns in between. The chance to see a bear or and elk in the wild, to see the wonders of nature brings them all. They almost always have a good time, and some are lucky enough to have an adventure while they are at it. I suppose that it is the same for all our national parks.

This fascinating sampling of the population shows me that, indeed, all kinds of people love our national parks. Perhaps it is not a statistically significant sample, but year after rainy year, there we are, a cross-section of America enjoying our national treasures. In the Great Smokies, the city slickers and hillbillies together jump into the Midnight Hole. Young and old hike the trails. Rich and poor set up camp in the campground. Wherever they come from, whatever their reason for visiting a national park, and what they do when they get to the park, they are us, in all our manifestations.

In 2014, we got to Big Creek in May, a month earlier than we had before. The leaves were not completely out yet so we could see more sky than we had in the past. It was 51 degrees when Andy checked the next morning about seven o'clock. I made oatmeal for breakfast and we sat outside at the picnic table to eat while we listened to birds and watched the morning sun shining through the leaves.

I saw a stunning wildflower part way around the campground. As I was taking a picture, Andy said there were some growing next to the motorhome. I hadn't seen them there. I'd never seen them anywhere. They were all over the place. I could hardly walk without stepping on them. I looked them up on the park website and learned they are yellow trillium and frequently seen in the lower elevations of the park. Big Creek is at about 1,800 feet. They are eight or twelve inches tall and the flower is about six to ten inches across.

On our first tour of the campground of the season, we chatted with the two men from Chattanooga in Site 10. They had a lot of questions: where to fish, where to get ice, could we make change so they could pay for another night? It was pleasant chatting with them, but I was anxious to get started on a wildflower hunt. The yellow trillium had inspired me. We followed the path by the creek down to the bridge. I was stopping and stooping every few feet to take another picture. My walking stick really came in handy to balance me when I squatted and was essential for me to stand back up. I renamed it my Standing-Back-Up Stick. Most of the flowers we saw were small. A few of them were incredibly tiny. The forest floor along Baxter Creek trail was covered with all manner of small wildflowers I had never seen before. Little wonders of nature lined the trail. Then I understood why the Smokies are called the wildflower national park and was overwhelmed with the need to preserve them for all of us.

We could hear Spence weed whacking in the distance first thing in the morning and we were eating lunch before he showed up at the RV. He was in mourning. His father had died some weeks before. Then, Sharon died two weeks later. His father's will had not been read yet, but the siblings were already feuding over the farm. I could only imagine the stress and sadness he was feeling.

Boss Larry showed up late in the afternoon, on his day off, to bring us park radios. He apologized for not being there when we arrived and making us feel forgotten. We knew he would show up eventually, but I was sure not expecting him on his day off. Larry always went above and beyond.

- *The first thing we heard on the park radio in the morning, other than rangers checking in, was a motorcycle accident with the rider on the ground. A park employee called it in, and he sounded distressed. He thought it was a chest injury, maybe a broken rib. He reported that the man was awake and alert. A few minutes later he plaintively asked when the emergency vehicle would be there. Once a ranger and the ambulance arrived, we did not hear any more about it. Dispatch called to ask if he should order a wrecker, but the ranger on the scene said other riders in the pack took care of the bike.*

- *A woman had locked herself out of her car at Newfound Gap. A park worker reported that she did not have a coat on and it was pretty cold up there. Dispatch called a VP (Volunteer in Park) who said they could help, but they were at least half an hour away. Later, after the VP had time to get there, dispatch reported that the woman had managed to get into her car.*

- *Two women in their fifties fell off the trail and were fifty feet down a steep bank. Dispatch asked about injuries. One woman probably had a broken thumb; the other was bleeding on her head. It seemed they were tangled in tree limbs and couldn't get back up to the Trillium Trail. A few minutes later a park employee reported he was with the women and they were going to walk out.*

- *In the early afternoon there were three separate reports of bears alongside the road. Two of them mentioned a bear with two cubs. There is a bear team that specializes in keeping the bears from getting hit by cars and shooing them away from campgrounds and picnic areas. One thing about referring to the bear as 350 always makes me laugh. The wildlife people who chase bears are numbers 351, 352, etc. So, according to the typical government organization chart numbering system, 350, the bear, is their supervisor.*

Boss Larry delivered our uniform shirts and fleece jackets, as well as the materials we needed to campground host. He and Andy went to the campground to empty the iron ranger. They brought the envelopes back to the RV where we counted them on the picnic table. I noticed a couple of envelopes were not sealed and did not have money in them. One envelope had "IOU $14" written on it. I was the witness and signed that Larry had counted them correctly. Larry just barely managed to stuff them all into a plastic envelope. As Larry was heading to his car he said over his shoulder something like, "If you need anything, call somebody who will listen." It was a joke, but close to the truth. He is stationed a long way from Big Creek and we were pretty much on our own. The rangers were also working on the more populous side of the park. If there was a real emergency, we just called dispatch on the radio and they sent rescue or an ambulance. Otherwise, we just dealt with the everyday problems as best we could.

Spence came by in the afternoon. He spent some time telling us what a wonderful wife Sharon had been and told a few humorous stories about her. Before she had become ill, she was a beautiful redhead. When she was a child, her mother entered her into a contest and she was one of the Little Miss Sunbeams on the bread wrappers.

- *A 57-year-old woman fell off a trail early in the day. Apparently, she only fell about three feet, but broke her leg. The person reporting it said it was the lower leg, just below the knee. Her leg was distorted. She must have been a long way up because the rescue went into the evening. They had to send a ranger to respond first. He put a splint on her leg. Then he requested a rescue crew with a litter to carry her out. There were several calls for dispatch to call the doctor to approve pain drugs. He asked for approval to give an injection, but the doctor only approved oral medication. They gave her pain medicine at least twice on the way down the trail. He requested a non-emergency transport to be at the trailhead to take her to the hospital.*

- *Dispatch called for a ranger to investigate a motor vehicle accident at Clingman's Dome. He didn't know whether it was one or two cars or if anyone was hurt, but there was something about a mountain lion. Maybe it was something in his voice that led Andy to remark, "Maybe he meant someone was lyin' on the mountain." I looked it up on the park web site in the evening and found out why dispatch sounded skeptical.*

"Scientists believe that the bobcat is the only wild feline that lives in the park. Visitors occasionally report seeing mountain lions; however, no concrete scientific evidence of their existence (such as tracks, scat, or other signs) has been found in the area in nearly thirty years." I didn't know the difference between a mountain lion and a bobcat until I looked them both up with Google Images. Perhaps all those mountain lion sightings are made by people as ignorant as me.

Andy was sitting up in the front seat looking out the window with his morning coffee when he saw a group of four or six turkeys in the group site. Before I could get the camera ready, the turkeys had ambled into the underbrush. I didn't even get a bird butt. After he laughed at my scrambling, Andy asked, "What do you call a group of turkeys?" and I found a great web site by the U.S. Geological Survey to answer that question for all kinds of animals. A group of turkeys is called a rafter or a gang.

- *A motorcycle rider from Indiana was down in the road. Park personnel had traffic stopped and emergency vehicles were on the way.*

- *A park worker requested that the electric company turn the power off in Cataloochee because a tree had fallen on a power line and was down on Palmer Road. They could not cut up the tree with live power lines on it. They also asked for someone to come help direct traffic while they worked. The callers were assigned the job of holding up traffic until the electric company arrived.*

- *In the evening, there was another motorcycle crash near Newfound Gap where a 58-year-old man flew over the guardrail and went down an embankment. He was lying about ten feet off the road. One ranger requested a technical rescue team and extraction tools. Another said the man was conscious and had pain in a leg and his back. It had been three years since we were campground hosts and monitored the park radio, but I recognized Ranger Heath's voice immediately. They called for the Life Star helicopter. A park rescue vehicle transferred the patient from the accident site to the helicopter landing zone.*

At about eight o'clock, two young men, probably college age, drove up in a car looking for the campground. I gave them directions and ten minutes later, they came back to say the campground was full. That surprised us as there were several empty sites when we walked around at five. They were heading east so I suggested they find a site in the Pisgah National Forest at the Harmon Den exit about seven miles east on the interstate. After they left, I thought that maybe I should have just told them to pitch their tent on the uninhabited group site for the night. They were going to be looking for a campsite in the pitch-black dark. I fretted about them all night.

At eight-thirty, I heard footsteps on the gravel outside and went out to find a German couple who had been on a longer hike than they anticipated and couldn't figure out where to find their car. He pointed to the ranger station on the map and I told them they just had another mile to go. This time, since it was already pitch-black dark out there, I offered to drive them down the road. They declined the offer and hiked away.

I turned off the lights at eleven o'clock and realized it was not dark outside. I could see car headlights over in the group camp so I turned on the porch light, got my flashlight and walked over. I was met by a young woman who said the campground was full. They were backpacking the next morning and needed a place to stay. Her husband was in the car trying to reserve the group site on his phone. I don't know if he succeeded, but told her that if he didn't, they could pitch their tents at the group site and be out early in the morning. I wasn't going to send two parties out in the dark of night.

- *The talk in the early morning was about a wildfire near the Rainbow Falls Trail. One man went up Mount LeConte to attempt to locate the fire. Another was walking down the Rainbow Falls trail. Yet another was closing off the trailhead with traffic cones and barriers. We heard them say they were taking Heath off night duty to help out. I also heard mention that the fire was spotted and reported by a private plane pilot flying over the park in the night. One person was assigned to investigate and was taking down the license plate numbers of the cars at the trailhead.*

Maintenance woman Linda from the Cosby campground was cleaning the campground toilet building on Spence's day off. I asked her about the light bulb in the ladies room that had been out for days. She said they did not have any spare bulbs and do not keep a supply on hand. Everyone was busy getting ready for the mountain festival at Cosby the next week and no one had time to run to the store for a bulb.

Linda worked in the Cosby campground, but would often come to clean the restrooms in Big Creek on Spence's days off. On weekends, Spence and Linda would work as a team, cleaning Cosby in the morning and Big Creek in the afternoon. Linda is also a local who lives in Cosby, TN. Like Spence, Linda is quite conscientious about her work and does a thorough job. She is also one of the sweetest women I've ever met.

- *Heath reached the wildfire shortly before noon. He said there was a lot of smoke. Then he asked for a weather report as he was getting light rain. About noon someone said they needed some status information for the public information office. The park was getting a lot of calls about the fire. It was nearly two in the afternoon when a ranger gave a report on the fire saying it was about ten to fifteen acres. He asked for lodging at the LeConte Lodge for the night for five people on the fire team. When the answer came back that there was room in the lodge, he asked if there was food with those rooms. The afternoon rains must have slowed down the fire because the fire crew walked out and cancelled their dinner plans at the lodge.*

- *A woman called to say that friends on the Mount Cammerer horse trail texted her to say a horse had fallen off the trail. They were asking for people to send ropes to pull the horse up. Ranger Jared was on the radio discussing the horse as I poured my morning coffee. They were planning to take some more horses and ropes up the trail to pull the fallen horse up. Jared was saying they had contacted some people in Bryson City, NC who had experience with this sort of thing, but the other park employee on the radio (618) should tell the man it might be in the afternoon or even the next day before help would be there. I wondered how the man fared out on the trail through the cold rainy night. Were he and the horse hungry? Jared told 618 to also tell the man that, other than getting in touch with the people in Bryson City, there was nothing else the park could do to help the man and his horse. I wondered how often a horse falls off a trail in the park...*

It was sixty degrees and raining, not a steady downpour but now soft, a pause, then harder all morning long. Most of the campers had tarps hung up to shelter them from the rain.

- *There must have been enough rain to put out the wildfire. At 1:55 someone reported that there was no longer any smoke coming from it.*

Spence and Linda dropped by to check on us in the afternoon. Somehow the subject of cat-head biscuits came up. That was something I never heard of and it called for some research. Spence and Linda described them as extra-large biscuits and the web sites I found surmised they are called cat head because they are as large as a cat's head.

- *Someone had fallen out of a tree at the Chimneys picnic area. When a ranger got there, he reported that the patient was on the ground on an island in the river. He was conscious, but not alert. Dispatch limited radio traffic to emergency only. One ranger drove up the road, and presumably across a bridge, to see if he could access the patient from the opposite side of the river. Later, he reported that it was impossible. He called for Rescue One. He also called for a crew with ropes to come set up a highline to get the patient across the river. An ambulance arrived to carry the patient to the Life Star helicopter, which landed at the Sugarlands Visitor Center.*

- *As we were walking back toward the motorhome, we heard a ranger checking in with dispatch. As the law enforcement rangers pull a vehicle over, they report the license plate number to dispatch. Dispatch tells them immediately who the owner of the vehicle is and whether they have violations or are "clear." When the ranger gets the driver's license from the driver, they call it in to dispatch too. That day, the dispatcher wanted to check that number again, but had entered it correctly. Yes, that license had expired on September 30, 2008! The driver had a number of past and outstanding issues with the law. Two-thousand-and-eight; are you kidding me? That was almost six years! A bit after this we heard that the vehicle was being towed to Cherokee. I wondered whether they arrested the man, gave him a ride to civilization, or just left him standing on the side of the road.*

- *Dispatch called for a ranger to investigate a woman on the road in a wheel chair a short distance out of Gatlinburg. That would be dangerous, even if she had a motor on that thing, with all the cars going over the speed limit on a curvy road with no shoulders. The ranger called back later to say the woman was staying "pretty well" off the road. She lived nearby.*

- *A few minutes later, a park visitor on horseback reported that he came across a hiker who had chopped his finger off. The horseback rider rode down the trail for cell phone coverage to report the incident. He told dispatch the man had a towel and duct tape around his hand. A ranger went up to investigate and the man was taken away in an ambulance.*

A young woman came in looking for a campsite after dark. I told her the campground was full and to use one of the group site spots. I gave her a money envelope and she set up her tent in the dark. I had softened up and didn't want to turn people away late in the day. Besides, the park needs the money.

On our next run to the grocery store, we went east to Waynesville, NC. I picked up some White Lily self-rising flour and a tub of lard for some biscuit experiments. I thought lard came in one-pound blocks like butter. But Ingles only had huge tubs. You gotta do what you gotta do for research. I bought the smaller size, a two-and-a-half pound tub.

- *A 58-year-old man had collapsed while hiking on the Ramsey Cascades trail. We had not heard the beginning and did not know what was going on, but the rescue involved ropes, a litter, helmets, and safety glasses. They closed down radio traffic except for the rescue team. There were thunderstorms in the area and the helicopter pilot was concerned about making the pickup. We heard him on the park radio checking on the weather at the landing zone. They later decided they could not fly to the University of Tennessee in Knoxville and would drive the patient in the ambulance. When it was over, there was a request that all members of the rescue team be interviewed as soon as they reached the trailhead. They also wanted statements from any witnesses. I wondered if something had happened to make this different than the other rescues we had listened to. Like the other rescues we had listened to that week, it was five hours after a person was hurt on the trail, word was given to park personnel, rangers arrived at the scene and made a rescue, transferred the patient to an ambulance or helicopter, that the patient was taken to the hospital. The wilderness is no place to get sick or have an accident requiring immediate medical attention. Later, my sister Barbara suggested that the man may have died. That would explain the need for statements from witnesses and rescue personnel.*

All that biscuit research inspired me to attempt biscuits like my Grandma used to make in Duplin County in eastern North Carolina. I remembered watching her make them using only flour, lard, and buttermilk. I distinctly recalled the beat-up metal flat-bottomed bowl she used to mix them up. After extensive internet research on southern biscuits for several days, I figured out why grandmothers never measured anything. It doesn't matter. There are recipes with varying ratios of flour, lard, and buttermilk. Whatever the ratio, within reason, you're gonna get biscuits.

After reading dozens of Mama's or Grandma's biscuit recipes, I came across one that reminded me most of <u>my</u> Grandma. What really clinched the choice for me was the bowl. The one pictured in the blog was the same bowl I had in the motorhome and it was one I got from my Mama's house. That was a sign from the biscuit goddess. However, the next morning I could not find the same blog. I used the recipe on the White Lily flour bag. Actually, I used the ratios. They call for Crisco and Grandma would have none of that, so I stuck with the lard. They were the best biscuits Andy had ever eaten. But then, he is a New York City boy and probably never had a real Grandma homemade southern biscuit. They were good, but they were not like my Grandma's.

Black Swallowtail butterflies appeared. I saw a cluster of them on the bank of the creek and a group in the day-use parking lot licking up dumped out soda or beer. We also saw them cluster on horse poop and pee spots. A group of butterflies is called a kaleidoscope. Perfect.

I had suggested that we walk around the campground three times a day to better check for food left out. There was none. We met Mary Ann and Larry from South Carolina who remembered us from a previous year and chatted with them for a bit. She told us a story of an older woman who camps there every year. A bear sliced through her tent during the night and snatched a pair of dirty socks. Apparently, the older woman was most chagrined over having socks so smelly that they attracted a bear. Bill Stiver, a Supervisory Wildlife Biologist in the Park, told me the sock-stealing bear was euthanized. Although stealing socks does not seem like a capital offense, it would only have been a matter of time before that bear hurt someone. How did they know which bear it was? Was it wearing the socks?

We had a gentle rain all night and there was no sunshine in the morning. Even so, the campers in five sites said they were staying another night. Everyone seemed dry and happy. The Indian couple in Site 10 thanked us for directing them to Wal-Mart for a tarp. They got it up just in time.

It was the second day of the biscuit experiment. I spent some time on the internet the night before until I found the site with my bowl. The blog, Taste of Southern, written by Steve Gordon, was entertaining as well as mouthwatering. Since there were only two of us, I planned to halve the recipe. Some days you just have a senior moment or two. Or, maybe this was a cook's moment. It happens. The recipe called for one-and-a-half cups of buttermilk. Half of that is three quarters. No problem with the math. But when I poured the buttermilk into the two-cup measuring cup, I had that moment and poured to the one-and-three-quarters line. I realized I had done wrong just as I poured it into the flour. There was so much buttermilk! The only thing to do was add more flour. How much? Until the batter turns to dough. Gosh, with more buttermilk and more flour, it needed more lard. Grab another glob and squish it in. Oh dear, you're not supposed to work the dough too much. More flour! These biscuits are not going to turn out right! Andy was worried my biscuits were going to be the BEST EVER and I would not know how much of any ingredients I used and would never be able to replicate them. I filled the whole pizza pan with huge biscuits. My convection-microwave oven only goes up to 450 degrees, not the called for 500 so I gave them some extra time because they were so large and I didn't want dough in the middle. They turned out fine. This experiment proves my hypothesis that it doesn't matter how much of each ingredient you put in, you're gonna get biscuits.

Sally in Site 2 had gone to Sevierville and bought a cooking tripod with a cast iron pot. She was cooking a big meal of beef stroganoff to share with some other campers when we walked by in the evening. Sally was joyous and said she felt like a pioneer woman tending the pot over a campfire.

Heath dropped by during one of the rain episodes. He had Backcountry Ranger Devin (424) with him and introduced us. I offered them hot chocolate and then asked, "What happened to that horse that fell off the trail?" As luck would have it, Ranger Devin was the one who went up the trail to assist the man and his horse. Devin was happy to tell the story.

Her name was Lucy and she was a beautiful chocolate brown quarter horse. The trail was narrow, just wide enough for a horse to walk. She apparently got a little spooked by something and then stepped too close to the edge of the trail and the ground gave way. She slid about 120 feet down a steep slope. Devin said you could see the path of destruction where she slid down. She was lucky she did not hit any trees, as she was going pretty fast on the steep mountainside. She came to a stop on a small level spot "about as big as a table." I suppose her rider jumped or fell off before sliding down with her.

Devin spent the night on the mountain with Lucy and her owner. He said they did not sleep on the little ledge with the horse, but put their sleeping bags on the trail above her. The man was not prepared for spending the night and was only wearing jeans and a t-shirt. Devin had taken a sleeping bag up the trail for him.

The next morning, they used a rope to lead Lucy back up the mountain to the trail. They took a long diagonal route rather than straight up and tried to keep her attention uphill rather than down. He said "encouragement" was required a few times. Devin said sometimes he was walking on the downhill side of the horse and was looking up at her belly. He was worried she would stumble and fall on him and they would both go sliding down the mountain. Sometimes she would get motivated and go so fast they had a hard time keeping up with her. His shoulder was against her and he could feel her warmth and flexing muscles. I asked Devin if he was a horse person and he replied that he was getting to be. I bet Lucy's owner considered him a hero.

Ranger Devin Phillips was young, in his twenties, tall and slender with fair hair and a boyish face. He was exceedingly polite and eager to tell his story. We never saw him again after that evening. He transferred to Black Canyon of the Gunnison National Park in Colorado.

Devin was a Back Country Ranger. He spent days at a time walking trails. He might remove small trees from the trail, or report larger ones to the trail crews. He checked the backcountry campsites to make sure campers had permits, were obeying the rules and staying safe. He might pick up the trash some hikers have left behind.

- *From Clingman's Dome: "We have snow showers up here." It was not my imagination; I heard that word twice. The temperature where we were, at 1,800 feet, never reached sixty degrees. I was glad we weren't any higher.*

Things were pretty quiet up at the tent campground in the evening. After we got back to the motorhome and I was rustling up some grub, the woman from the horse camp knocked on the door with two grilled chicken breasts. She had prepared them for another couple who had reserved the site next to them, but they didn't show up. What a treat; dinner delivered in the forest.

Spence and Linda drove up with a pickup truck loaded with firewood the next morning. They had been cutting up storm-damaged trees over at the Cosby campground and there were plenty of log segments lying on the ground over there. Spence said Linda made him do it; he would have only brought two pieces if she had not been on his back. I put on a fresh pot of coffee while Andy and Spence unloaded the wood.

The cold, wet weather, and the end of the weekend must have meant there were not so many people in the park. It was a rare day without any rescue dramas on the radio. Most of the calls to dispatch were traffic related. There were an unusually large number of calls to report bears and elk though. There were several calls about a hurt or sick bear near the edge of the road. It was sluggish and curled up next to a tree. The rangers apparently tried to shoo the bear farther into the woods so it would not back up traffic and cause a bear jam. If I kept my bears straight, it eventually climbed a tree and went back to sleep. Another bear was sleeping on a branch overhanging the road. The ranger reported that people driving under the branch didn't seem to notice it. There were several bear jams. Moreover, there must have been five or six calls just to report a bear's location. Some park personnel no doubt rushed to the scene to chase the bear into the woods, or at least keep the park visitors from getting too close while taking pictures. Spence said there were more bears in the park than ever before.

We didn't usually hear that much about elk. That day there were three radio calls concerning them. There was an elk jam. At one point someone reported an injured elk. Rangers are continuously giving warnings and tickets for people speeding in the park. The elk and bears suffer when people speed. Late in the day, someone reported a herd of elk in the road they could not shoo off. A wildlife specialist went to assist. I suppose an elk stands pretty much wherever he wants to. That brings to mind an important question. How do you annoy an elk just enough so that he wanders off into the woods rather than stomp you to death?

The other radio traffic we had been hearing for several days was about trees fallen across the road. Someone reported it and road crews dashed out with chain saws. If the tree was small enough, they would simply drag it off the road. There were always more fallen trees after a heavy rain.

8

Rain

I have seen those weather systems sweeping west to east across the country on the Weather Channel. Then I picture those clouds bumping into the Appalachian Mountain Range. All of them are not high enough to float above the mountains so they build up on the western side. Others get hung up on the mountain tops like a tuft of lamb's wool on a thistle. Then, the puffy white clouds from children's drawings turn dark and threatening. When enough of them have amassed, they pour their insides out and onto the Smoky Mountains, turning parts of it into a temperate rain forest. Of course, they don't describe it exactly like that on the Weather Channel.

Most campers are hardy folks who don't let a little, or even a lot, of rain ruin their parade or their camping trip. The serious, regular campers are prepared for it. They have good tents with flies and hang tarps over their campsite to protect them from the rain when they are not sleeping in the tent. They sit around the campfire under their tarp as comfortable and dry as ever. Others, new campers or those who cannot afford the fancy equipment, get wet. All their clothes and bedding get wet too. They react to it in different ways.

Some, especially those with children, pack up and leave right away to go home. I don't blame them. I wouldn't want to be cooped up in a tent all day with a couple of rambunctious kids either. There is at least one campsite with clotheslines laden with clothes and sleeping bags after a rainy night. Even some of the most experienced campers and backpackers head for home when it rains every day of their stay. That is not what they come to the mountains for. A few *times, campers headed to a motel for the night and dried their belongings in a laundromat. Then, they returned to the tent for the next night.*

How many of them know how often it rains in the park before planning their trip? A quick stop at the hardware or camping store for a tarp or two could make the difference between comfort and a cold sog. A large tarp above the tent will keep even an old tent dry. So many of them are not really prepared for it. Maybe they don't expect it, either from ignorance or optimism. A twenty-percent chance of rain doesn't sound like much.

A beautiful weather forecast cannot be relied on in the Smoky Mountains. Even a rainy forecast might not apply to Big Creek. The mountainous terrain diverts those rain clouds unexpected ways. We have heard Dispatch announce approaching storms with high winds and heard the thunder over the other side of the mountain while we stayed dry and calm.

I love the rain. We walk around in the pouring rain with our raincoats and I always carry a large umbrella to keep the camera dry. There are not many places where water collects since we are on a sloping mountainside, so our shoes don't get wet. All the leaves in the forest are dancing to their own drumbeat. Everything is shiny and clean, except the mud running down the side of the road to our host site. The smell of the forest is enhanced. When it rains harder, the sound of Big Creek is diminished or obscured completely. The best part is when the sun comes back out after a passing shower and the forest sparkles. I feel fresh, and new, and clean.

After it rains in Big Creek, or elsewhere near us, we go check the water level in the creek. There is always white water tumbling down the mountain, but after a heavy rain, Big Creek rises and becomes a torrent of white. We must raise our voices to talk when we stand on the bridge in the picnic area.

Even on the coldest, rainiest weekends, there will be campers in the Big Creek tent campground. They come to experience whatever the mountains have to offer, rain or shine.

We headed to Newport, TN for our weekly shopping trip. Strawberries were on sale so I bought a large package. That reminded me. We didn't have strawberry shortcake when I was a child. My mother made biscuits. She would slice up the strawberries, add sugar and then stick her hands into the bowl and squish them up "real good" so there was plenty of juice. She put a biscuit in a bowl and covered it with squished strawberries. When I later discovered shortcake, I was sorely disappointed. After we got home, I whipped up another batch of biscuits and squished some strawberries. We ate them outside by the campfire after we did our evening campground walkaround.

- *There was a medical emergency at the Collins Creek pavilion. When a ranger got there, he reported that the patient was blue and people were administering CPR. They took the patient by ambulance to Cherokee.*

- *A car towing a trailer lost its brakes and was stopped in a construction zone and blocking traffic in both directions. Dispatch ordered a tow truck.*

- *BOLO for a man in a black Chevy pickup, possibly with bullet holes in the side of it. He had been involved in a homicide and was thought to be heading for either Tennessee or Michigan. The family had reported that he was heavily armed and dangerous. Sometime later dispatch made the announcement again and asked each ranger in service to respond, to confirm that he or she got the message.*

- *A bear with two cubs was in a tree at least fifty feet above the ground between a campground and a picnic area. The man on the scene said he had pyrotechnics and asked if he should use them to try to scare the bear away. The response was just to keep the park visitors far enough away so the bear could come down out of the tree if she wanted to and he would assess the situation when he got there.*

Pyrotechnics? I had to Google that. Park personnel try to chase bears away by making loud noises including using air horns. They will shoot small fireworks toward the bear. They will even shoot the bear with paint balls, which will also mark the bear. So if you see a bear in the Smokies wearing tie dye, it is not a hippie bear from the sixties, but a bear that has been hanging around a campground looking for picnic baskets and coolers that ended up on the losing end of a paintball fight with a wildlife specialist.

- *A man was on the trail near Clingman's Dome with a twisted ankle and could not walk. A ranger said he was on the way with some crutches. Later, the ranger reported that the ankle was blue and swollen. The man was between 200 and 250 pounds. He was less than a mile along the trail so they were hoping he could crutch himself out.*

- *BOLO for an extremely intoxicated man driving a Ford Focus from Gatlinburg to Pigeon Forge with a small child in the car. A ranger reported that he was in a position to watch for the car, but we never heard any more about it unless it was one of the many calls for a registration and driver's license check.*

The man from Site 3 showed up in his car with the remainder of their firewood. He said they decided to give it to us because we had been so nice and helpful to them while they were camping. If they had left it on Site 3, it would have been Steve and Ginger's campfire that night.

Steve and Ginger saw us coming and walked to greet us with hugs and hellos. They had been camping there enough years to know you need to get there early in the morning to be sure to get a campsite. They had driven from Cincinnati the day before and spent the night at a motel in Newport so they could be waiting for a choice campsite to open up in the morning.

We left for the season kick-off employee picnic at the Twin Creeks Pavilion in Gatlinburg. The speeches had started when we got there; Andy noted that we had arrived too early. The outgoing, interim, park superintendent, referred to by all as Pedro, was giving a farewell speech. This was his last day. It was immediately clear why he was well liked. He was positive, cheerful, enthusiastic, warm and sincere.

Pedro had been walking around the pavilion and chatting with most people. He stopped at our table and we talked for a few minutes. He told us he was the Superintendent of the Big Cypress National Preserve, one of our favorite destinations in the Everglades. He thanked us for our volunteer efforts and I assured him we like it so much that the park should be charging us for the opportunity. He bent down, leaned in close, and whispered, "I know what you mean. I often feel embarrassed when I get my paycheck."

The campground was a buzz of activity. The holiday weekend had begun. Hopeful campers arrived early to take over a site as soon as someone else left. I call them hoverers. Several had already put their pay stubs on the board underneath the current camper's stub. We spent nearly three hours at the campground chatting with people, giving the bear lecture, answering questions, giving hiking information, and making sure everyone was settled in well. I was happy to see Boss Larry drive up to the registration station. He said he was happy to have us there.

- *A woman at Rainbow Falls fell and got a one-and-a-half-inch gash on her forehead above her brow. A physician happened to be there and fashioned a make-shift bandage. They were walking out, but the physician thought someone should meet them on the trail to assess her condition.*

There must have been a lot of scattered clouds whipping across the sky. It was as though the sun was blinking on and off, like a fluorescent light bulb when it is about to burn out. One minute it would be dark enough to start raining and the next minute the sun would be brilliant. Although we thought it imminent, we never did get rain after the early morning shower.

An exhausted man with a big pack on his back came searching the campground for a campsite in the evening. He was shockingly thin and haggard. I told him the campground was full. He had hiked all day and needed a place to camp. I wasn't sure whether he was confused or simply exhausted. We told him to come pitch his tent on our site and Andy showed him the way while I finished walking around the campground. When I got back, his tent was set up next to the horse trail. I decided to talk to him a bit to make sure he was alright.

He was Joe from Newton, Massachusetts. He had spent the past ten days hiking the Benton MacKaye trail through the national park. He had eaten the last of his food in the morning and hiked about ten or eleven miles and down 4,000 feet that day. I offered him a peanut butter and jelly sandwich and the remainder of the Caprese salad we had for dinner. He was anxious to make a phone call to reserve a back-country site for the next night. I handed him a granola bar. He said he needed to go to the ranger station to get his car so I offered to drive him down there. The man clearly had done enough hiking for the day. There was no cell phone signal at the ranger station or in the motorhome so I called dispatch on the radio and asked if he could help me make a reservation for the man. He said he would try. Joe sat on the couch eating with gusto.

On most evenings, the radio traffic drops off sharply after five o'clock. That night, rangers were calling 700 every minute. Of course, their business stopping errant drivers, etc. takes priority over making a back-country reservation. Every time a ranger called in with a license plate or driver's license number, I had to stand by while 700 looked it up and reported back to the ranger. They were calling in one after the other. At one point, a ranger came on the radio and told dispatch to wait until their business was complete before continuing with the camping permit. We waited and waited. Finally, after half an hour, the ranger came back on to report his incident to 700 and get a case number. When that was done, 700 called me immediately to finish up Joe's back-country camping permit. Joe had finished his salad and sandwich and looked somewhat revived. He told us he had been wearing the same pants for the last ten days to keep the weight of his pack down. Then he started telling jokes. His favorite, which we had already heard, was "How do you distinguish black bear and grizzly bear scat? The grizzly scat is the one with the little bells in it."

Being the scientist he is, Andy could hardly bear the thought of suspending the great biscuit experiments. He decided to set up his own test by making biscuits himself while I was showering. He set out to prove, or disprove, my stated hypothesis; "It doesn't matter how much of each ingredient you put in, you're gonna get a biscuit."

Andy's test was as so: He put half a cup of flour and half a cup buttermilk into a bowl and mixed them together. Then he added a large serving spoon of lard into the mix. He mixed some more (with a large spoon; he didn't want to get his hands yucky) and kept adding flour a bit at a time until he decided the dough consistency was right to form biscuits. It was sticky. Still not wanting to get his hands gooey, he dropped the dough onto the pizza pan with a serving spoon and put the pan into the oven. He fried four slices of bacon to a crisp while the biscuits were baking. I was dressed at this point and came to the kitchen to observe. When the biscuits looked about right to Andy, he asked me to pull them out of the oven. He had four large biscuits. We put two on each plate and set out to analyze the test results. The biscuits were delicious. They were better than all the ones I had made. I think his lard proportion was higher than mine, and getting closer to Grandma Dorothy. The test results, according to Andy, were that he verified my hypothesis. "You're gonna get a biscuit." There is a wide range of possible ratios of flour, buttermilk, and lard.

- *A jeep had parked too close to the edge of the road and was tipped over so far that it was nearly rolling over. No one was in the vehicle and it was not damaged. Dispatch called for a wrecker to come pull it out.*

Heath and Devin arrived to hike up the Big Creek trail. Later, we could hear Heath on the radio calling in to make reservations for campers without backcountry permits. I noticed that Heath got it done much faster than I did.

- *A woman fell twenty to thirty feet and had facial, leg, and other injuries. The emergency medical services were on the scene in just a few minutes. They were calling for a litter and were "preparing the package for transport."*

- *A car was left running with the ignition taped in the on position. There was no one around so a ranger went to check it out.*

- *A few minutes before eight, a teenage boy and girl had not returned from the trail and were last seen four or five hours before. The rangers organized to hike up the various trails in the vicinity to look for them. At 8:20, dispatch reported that there was a phone call from the mother and she had heard from the kids.*

The next morning, Andy cracked open the door to the bedroom, "Do you smell that?" Coffee. I grunted and covered my eyes. In what seemed only a few minutes later he was at the door again. "Do you smell that?" Bacon. I moaned and rolled over. A few minutes later he was at the door again. "Do you smell that?" No, I didn't detect any new smells. But it was nearly 8:00 so I rolled out of bed to see what he was up to. Biscuits. He had another batch of biscuits in the oven. He thought he would see whether he could replicate the test results from two days before. That's the scientific method. He wanted me to take them out of the oven again. They were small but beautiful. The bottoms had a delightful crispy golden crust. I put three on each bread plate and Andy garnished them with strips of bacon. Spence arrived and I gave him one of my biscuits and filled his coffee cup. The biscuits were delicious, though I thought he should have used salted butter to brush the tops.

The campground was almost emptied in the morning as the campers headed back home. Steve and Ginger's children had left at 7:00 for Washington, DC and they were beginning to pack up themselves. We stood around talking for a while, but eventually decided we were distracting them from packing and continued our walkaround.

We had had a rain shower early and then the sun shone intensely through the forest. The temperature was comfortably cool making a beautiful morning for a walk. The air above Big Creek was filled with some of that Smoky Mountain smoke, otherwise known as mist. It was frustrating that my pictures did not capture the brilliance, or the smell, or the humidity, or the sound of the creek rushing over the rocks.

Back at the motorhome, I began washing the breakfast dishes. The sink was full of scientific utensils, most of them covered with lard. There were three large serving spoons and several spatulas. I held up the thin, flexible metal one and asked him, "What did you use this one for?"

"For spreading the lard on the pizza pan."

"It's covered with lard!"

"Yeah, but my hands stayed clean. Mostly." We had been out for about two hours. When I got to the pizza pan on which the biscuits had been baked, the lard had cooled and returned from liquid back to the white grease that comes in the tub. The whole pizza pan was white.

"No wonder those biscuits had that nice brown crispy crust on the bottoms. You fried them in the oven!" I had to wash that pan twice to get all the grease off. Andy had gone way past Grandma Dorothy on the lard factor.

Heath had arrived to get the money from the iron ranger and picked up Andy to witness the process. When they finished, they came back to the RV so Heath could eat the piece of monthly birthday cake we had saved for him. Yes, I bake a birthday cake for Andy on the twenty-second of every month.

Heath was just leaving when Steve and Ginger arrived with their car packed for the trip back to Cincinnati. We drove two cars to Carver's Apple House in Cosby, TN. We didn't linger after the meal because they needed to get on the road, but it was such a pleasure to sit together and chat over a good meal.

- *A daughter called dispatch on the phone to say her mother had called her from the Deep Creek trail. The mother had seen a bear and went back up the trail and was now afraid to come down. She was not hurt. As near as I could figure, her mother wanted someone to come up and escort her down the trail. A ranger responded with a request for the girl's phone number. Bill Stiver, the park's Supervisory Wildlife Biologist, told me the bear had to be euthanized. If a bear is following a hiker, it is usually after some food and not necessarily out to attack the person. But following a person for food means the bear has lost its fear of humans and has become dangerous.*

Bear attacks are extremely rare. In 2010 Sean Konover, age 26, got too close to a bear while taking pictures. The bear bit him on the foot. In my opinion, Konover was at fault for getting too close, yet he only got a slight puncture requiring no medical attention. That bear was euthanized because the human was able to get too close. From the park web site; "Willfully approaching within fifty yards (150 feet), or any distance that disturbs or displaces a bear, is illegal in the park." I hoped Konover got a big fine in addition to his bear bite.

Bill Stiver had to think about it for a bit to remember bear attacks. He recalled three incidents where hikers who were sleeping out under the stars in the back country had been bitten by a bear. He mentioned an arm, a leg, and the buttocks. Buttocks? Holy crap! That would be a rude awakening. Bill also said that in 2001 a man was pulled out of his hammock at Elkmont. Two bears were hanging around the campground there and both of them were put down. He also recalled that a man was bitten on the arm while sleeping in a hammock in Big Creek. He said no one had been bitten by a bear while sleeping in a tent. I have always thought people sleeping in hammocks look like a big taco.

Spence told us about the first time he took Sharon camping when he was working on the trail crew. He brought Sharon to Big

Creek. He laughed as he told us she brought her hair blow dryer as there is no electricity available in the park. They had all their food stored properly in the truck. During the night, a rustling woke Spence. He was on high alert for bear activity when he realized the rustling was Sharon opening a candy bar she had tucked under her pillow for a late-night snack. As animated as Spence was telling this story, I can only imagine the bear-safety lecture he gave Sharon that night.

Camp Carolina, in the group site, had made three long tents with huge tarps, the blue or gray kind with grommets on the edges. The tents were at least twenty feet long. The peak of the tarp-tent was thigh-high to me. I didn't see it happen in the night, but imagine a guy lies down at the entrance on either end and rolls toward the center until he gets to another person. The one in the middle had better not need to get out during the night.

We had taken several days off to visit family. Spence stopped by to say welcome back and mentioned that someone had left a tent in the campground. When we walked around in the evening, I realized immediately which tent. Site 5. When they arrived on May 25, they had to go to Wal-Mart to buy some tent stakes. I had left courtesy notices several times for them for leaving food out while they were gone. We had not seen them for several days before we left. That is not uncommon; people go hiking. I decided to unzip the tent to make sure no one was inside sick, or worse. Thankfully, no one was in there. However, there was food, a cardboard box full of small bags of assorted chips and a bag of hamburger buns. There were two six packs of plastic soda bottles. We carried those to the bear-proof locker and saw the food we had put in before our trip still there. I found two notes on the picnic table. Two females had brought them some food in a plastic grocery bag and left it on the picnic table. It had apparently been there for several days. I could not decide from the notes whether they were left on the same or different days. The men had not paid for their campsite and their tab was no longer on the registration board.

I called dispatch on the telephone to report the unusual situation. He thought they were probably not hurt on the trail, because someone would have seen them by now. The park is that busy. I could only describe them vaguely, a man in his fifties or sixties and one in his thirties. They had come with a woman the week before they camped to check out the campground. We had chatted with them on the bridge. The young woman was with the younger man and they had just returned to the area, I presumed to be his home. The older man could have been his father. When they arrived on Sunday, the woman was with them. She told me she was pregnant and did not want to sleep in a tent. She stayed around most of the day and then left in the evening. I did not recall seeing the men again after that first day.

Spence came walking up to the motorhome and knocked on the door. His park truck would not start in the horse campground. He took the emergency battery jumper to get it started and then came back to heat his lunch in the microwave and eat at our picnic table.

The afternoon campground walkaround took over three hours. Ranger Chuck was supposed to come remove the tent and gear on Site 5, but it was still there. We asked everyone in the area if they had seen anyone on Site 5, but no one had.

Site 10 had no people but did have a cooler and plastic bin full of food sitting at the picnic table. There was a fire going in the fire pit. There were four insect-repelling candles burning around the perimeter of the campsite. A bag of trash was hanging on a tree. The white Styrofoam cooler was the worst. I took the rock off the top and looked inside. It was mostly ice so I stuck my hand in to see if it was just sodas or food. I felt a fish. Oh dear God, a Styrofoam cooler of fish. I filled out a courtesy notice. Unattended fire – check. Food storage violations – check. Sanitation violation (trash bag) – check. Ranger Chuck drove into the campground just as I was finishing the form. I met him at Site 5.

Andy said the people from Site 10 had returned. They had been gone for over two hours. Chuck went to give them a ticket while Andy and I folded up the tent on Site 5 and loaded it into the bag with the poles and stakes. Two guys looking for a campsite brought their gear and set it on Site 5, ready to set up as soon as it was clear. They helped carry the abandoned gear to Chuck's SUV. There was enough camping gear to fill it. Then we got the cooler and food we had stowed in the bear-proof locker. Chuck took the cooler, the box of bags of chips, and sodas and said to throw away the rest of the food.

- *BOLO. A man of questionable sanity, armed with a gun. The family had called police because they were worried he might hurt himself.*

- *A woman said she had jumped from a car in which she had been taken against her will. She was carrying two bags and said she did not have any money and did not know where to go. We heard dispatch and rangers discussing who was going to do what. They had a description of the car – white Jeep Wrangler. She was apparently not hurt. Some rangers were headed toward her, some were going to intercept the jeep. The reporting party did not think the woman was "100 percent, mentally." Maybe she was distraught. Later, the reporting party had lost contact with the woman. He was worried she was going to harm herself or someone else. I heard rangers reporting their positions. Then there was nothing more about it. Did they find her? Did they find the Jeep? Had she really been kidnapped or was she just crazy?*

I stayed awake that night. Chuck had told us a small baby bear had been run over by a car right at the exit ramp off I-40. I was still wondering what could have happened to the two men who never returned to Site 5. I could not think of any good reasons, only bad. What happened to the woman? Periodically, I wondered how the campers in Site 10 could have left all that food out, after hearing our excellent bear lecture.

I pondered the dispatcher's comment that if the men were hurt on a trail, someone would have seen them. Our experience was only in a front-county campground, one you can reach by car. They were full of people. I just assumed that a person could take a trail out into the back country and be completely alone. There are 800 miles of trails after all. Are there also 800 miles of hikers out there every day? If so, where is the wilderness? Yes, of course, the wilderness is off the trails where it is too easy to get disoriented and not find the trail again. I couldn't understand why someone would leave the established trail, but maybe the reason is to look for that solitude or real adventure they can't find otherwise.

I made another batch of biscuits for breakfast, this time to give Andy the biscuits-and-country-ham experience. He was surprised at the saltiness, but seemed to enjoy it. He observed that it made the coffee taste wonderful. That might have been my best batch of biscuits yet. I had learned some biscuit-making skills from lard-wielding Andy.

- *A ranger made a routine traffic stop for a tail light being out and when he gave the license number to dispatch, the report came back that the man had a warrant for his arrest for several crimes, one of which was embezzlement. The ranger took him to the jail in Cherokee.*

- *A park visitor reported a car off the road and twenty feet down an embankment with the rear of the car in the water. Dispatch called for emergency radio traffic only. The driver was reporting chest and leg pain, but he was awake and alert. Two rangers were directing traffic, alternating cars past the wreck site. They decided to get the Life Star helicopter to transport the patient, who was loaded into an ambulance at 6:44.*

- *First thing Friday morning, a woman had fallen a few feet down a slope less than a mile from the Deep Creek Campground. No head injuries. Leg swelling. EMS was on the way. A ranger called for the Deep Creek Camp Hosts or Maintenance to unlock the gate for an ambulance.*

I never ceased to be amazed at how many drivers who were stopped by the park rangers had expired driver's licenses or tags. We heard it nearly every day, often more than once a day.

9

Dogs

I love dogs. Just about everyone does. Even cat people love dogs. They aren't mere animals; they are part of the family. How many times have you said, or heard someone else say, "He doesn't know he's a dog; he thinks he is a person?" So, it is not surprising at all that when we go out for a walk in the woods, we take Fido along with us. Poor thing has been left home alone in the house all week and needs to get out and enjoy the outdoors as much as people do.

Here's the link to the site just in case you're thinking of visiting the Great Smoky Mountains and you want to bring your dog: http://www.nps.gov/grsm/planyourvisit/pets.htm. In summary, it says large national parks that have extensive backcountry areas as a rule do not allow dogs on trails. Great Smoky Mountains National Park has prohibited dogs in the backcountry since the park was first established in the 1930s. The park prohibits dogs on hiking trails for several reasons: Dogs can carry disease into the park's wildlife populations. Dogs can chase and threaten wildlife, scaring birds and other animals away from nesting, feeding, and resting sites. Dogs bark and disturb the quiet of the wilderness. Pets may become prey for larger predators such as coyotes and bears. Many people, especially children, are frightened by dogs, even small ones. Uncontrolled dogs can present a danger to other visitors.

Those seem like pretty good reasons to me to keep a dog away from the trails, and it doesn't even mention dogs getting bitten by snakes or dogs getting *into fights with each other. Both of those things happened while we were in the park.*

I am not surprised that people are not aware of the no-pets rule when they come to the park. People don't read rules and the signs are just a part of the scenery. I am not even surprised anymore at the number of people who choose to ignore the rule when we tell them pets are not allowed on trails. They decide to take the risk of getting a fine. In reality, it's not much of a risk; rangers don't hike up Big Creek Trail all that often. What does surprise me is how angry and offended many dog owners were when we told them pets are not allowed. They are the ones who make an angry remark and then huff on up the trail with Fido as though I was some pervert that just flashed them. I always imagine getting on the radio and calling for a ranger who will rush right over and give them a citation, but that's not going to happen.

Pets are allowed in the campgrounds, picnic areas, and along the roads. But the rules are pretty clear about this as well: they must be kept on a leash at all times, that leash can't be longer than six feet, and "pet excrement must be immediately collected by the pet handler and disposed of in a trash receptacle." And here's the biggie: "pets should not be left unattended in vehicles or RVs."

Sometimes I wonder if even having pets in the campgrounds and picnic areas is too much. The campsites are close together. Some dogs bark loud and often, annoying the neighbors. Even an overly-friendly dog frightens the rare non-dog-lover when their owner does not pay attention to the leash rules. I've seen more than one tiny lap-dog left out in a campsite as coyote bait.

I love dogs. I don't have a dog because it seems cruel to me to leave them inside a motorhome all day while we are out. I often have dog treats on hand to befriend other people's dogs though. After getting angry about people leaving their dogs unattended, I decided to do something about it. I began offering dog-sitting services to the hikers who did not want to break the park rules. Sometimes I really didn't want to give the dog back.

People want to bring their dogs with them to enjoy the experience of the great outdoors. Maybe the dog regulations are the reminder that this "great outdoors" is actually a very confined space, with people sleeping and relaxing not that far from where you are. We want our wilderness experience to be pristine, not restricted or hampered by rules (the definition of untrammeled.) That's the great myth of wilderness actually, but while our national parks are our reminder of the awesome grandeur of nature, the hard fact is, they are a piece of land bounded by civilization. And we must remember that when we come to them, we should bring our civility—our manners—with us.

I had seen two people leading llamas up the trail one morning, but they were already gone by before I could grab the camera. When they walked back down in the afternoon, I asked them to stop for pictures. They only paused a moment because some horses were coming down behind them, and horses made the llamas nervous. This was the first time we had seen llamas on the horse trail, but they are actually a common sight in the park if you are in the right place at the right time. A llama train takes supplies up the Trillium Gap Trail to the Mount LeConte Lodge three times a week. The lodge is only accessible on foot. They even have a regular schedule posted on the Mount LeConte Lodge web page. Search YouTube for a llama video with: "Mt. Le Conte Lodge Llama Train, Great Smoky Mountains."

We were almost finished with our afternoon walk around the campground when the woman from Site 1 approached us. They had driven her father's pickup truck up to Davenport Gap to hike on the Appalachian Trail in the afternoon. When they came back out to the road, their pickup truck was gone. As in stolen. She said the thieves must have taken it away with a tow truck because they could see marks on the ground where the pickup had been dragged. They called the park to report the theft. A Good Samaritan gave them a ride back to the campground where the daughter's car was parked.

This was another first for us and I felt really bad about the theft, as though it was somehow our fault. The old man was a World War II veteran. Three generations of the family had come down to the park from Indiana for a vacation. They could not get all five people and the camping gear into the car to drive home. They passed us in the lower parking lot and told us they were going down to the park entrance to make some phone calls. A day visitor overheard and asked us what had happened. When I told him, he responded, "That's Cocke County. That truck has probably already been stripped clean."

I was peeling and slicing peaches for a cobbler when we got a call on the radio from dispatch. He asked us to take the campers to the ranger station and call him on the telephone so he could start a report. He asked me if the vehicle had been parked on park property or across the road, which would mean it was in Cocke County and not park jurisdiction. I had thought to ask the woman that; the truck was across the road from the park and in Cocke County. We drove down the road heading out of the park to find them. It was easy. They were at the park entrance along with a Cocke County policeman. That was fast. I called 700 on the radio to report that the police officer was there, and 700 told me he didn't need to talk to the campers if Cocke County was taking care of it.

Cosby campground host Regina stopped by to say hello the next morning. As she got out of her car, she noticed there was a bird flying around inside the screen room. We opened the screen, but the bird didn't get the idea. I held one side open while Regina went to the back side to encourage the bird in the right direction. On the second "shoo," the bird flew out of the tent and grazed Andy's head as he came out of the RV. Shortly after Regina left, the man from Site 1, whose pickup was stolen, came to the door.

"Remember yesterday you said to ask if you could do something to help us?" I did.

"I thought of something. Do you have any way to store our camping gear until we can come back and get it in a couple of weeks?" I figured we could put it in the back room of the ranger station. Andy told him we would drive our car up to the campground for our morning walkaround and then, when they were ready, go with them to the ranger station to store their gear.

We drove to the campground, counted up the vacancies for the morning vacancy report, and then Andy walked around to the other sites while I went to check on the progress at Sites 1 and 5. Apparently the grandfather and grandson stayed in one site while his two daughters and granddaughter stayed in the other. That was two campsites, but they had enough gear for several more. The gear was piling up and, fortunately, the woman in Site 6 volunteered her big pickup truck to drive it all down the mountain. Andy and I went down to the ranger station to clear a spot. We designated the spot where they could put their gear and not block the ranger's rescue equipment or the door to the garage, which is Spence's domain.

The pickup arrived, piled high with camping gear. I directed the woman to back up as close to the door as possible. The grandson was sitting on top of the toolbox in the back of the truck. When they came to a stop, Grandpa's head popped up. He was lying on top of the tents. "Darn!" I had forgotten my camera and that was the picture of the day - missed.

We showed them where to pile their gear and they started with large plastic bins. Then they had a cooler, the two tents, tarps, numerous sleeping bags, poles, walking sticks, a footlocker they called their bear box, a smaller wooden box, and even a piece of fire wood. It was two pickup loads. Spence had arrived while they were back at the campground for the second load and we told him what was going on. "Yep, that's Cocke County. Was it a Chevy?" Yes, it was.

The next day, the radio was nonstop.

- *A white Mercedes was off the road on the northbound spur near King Branch and the lady had crawled up to the road from the vehicle. The reporting party could not see the car from the road. A Gatlinburg ambulance and fire truck were on the scene. The woman was not requesting an ambulance, but wanted medical assistance. Then, the woman would be taken to University of Tennessee hospital. The ranger called 700 to make sure the wrecker was prepared to get the car out of the river and thirty to forty feet up the vertical riverbank. Sometime later the ranger called to tell dispatch the woman had refused transport.*

- *A branch fell off a tree and hit an eleven-year-old boy across his back. The reporting park person thought the boy was OK, but shaken up. They wanted a ranger to come check on him. There was no ranger available, so dispatch called EMS from town. That was the first time we had heard them say no rangers were available. There was a lot going on in the park at the same time. The poor dispatch fellow got one call after the other in quick succession.*

That got me to wondering. Did the park have enough rangers? I only knew from my own observations. We had an unmanned ranger station in Big Creek. The closest station in Cosby was thirty minutes away and the rangers stationed there covered a lot more area in the opposite direction. Their range was huge. We had learned not to call for a ranger except in real emergencies; they just didn't have the time to drive all the way to Big Creek for a dog running free or a cooler left unattended. Some amateur research was in order.

I wondered how the number of law enforcement rangers in the Great Smoky Mountains National Park compares to a city police force. I found the number of park visitors on the park's web site and divided the July 2010 figure by 31 days to get 45,290 per day. Then I Googled a list of US cities ranked by population and found Wauwatosa, a suburb of Milwaukee, Wisconsin with a population of 45,004 according to the July 2008 census data. The city web site said there were 124 employees in the Police Department as of January 2015. The Great Smoky Mountains National Park Law Enforcement Division had 66 as of July 2014. Of course, my data comes from different dates, but, again, this is amateur analysis here. I divided the population by the law enforcement staff. Wauwatosa, Wisconsin has 363 people per police department staff member. The Great Smoky Mountains National park has 686 visitors per the Law Enforcement Division staff. Does it mean anything that Wauwatosa has almost twice as many officers per population than the park has law enforcement officers per visitors? Maybe, maybe not.

- *A "baby deer" was standing on the side of the road and attracting a crowd. A bit later, someone reported that the fawn and mama were reunited.*

- *People from Kentucky in a red Ford Explorer were having car problems. The driver's seat was all the way forward and would not go back. The man could not fit into the car to drive it. They wanted to be towed in the direction of Kentucky. Dispatch called a wrecker and then a while later, the ranger called dispatch to say they had moved the seat back and the family was on their way.*

One afternoon the campers from Texas stopped their car by us along the campground road as we were walking out. The young man asked us if there was a place with a good view. Of course, we told him Max Patch and gave him directions on how to get there. The next morning, the young man was standing near the registration board. He thanked us profusely for sending him to

Max Patch. It was perfect. The view was wonderful. They were the only ones there. He proposed marriage and she accepted. Andy said, "You don't have to tell us she accepted; we could see that from your big grin." When I asked, he said yes, she was surprised. Her family already knew. He had asked for her mother's and her brother's permission to marry her. He was standing there waiting for her to come out of the ladies room. He showed us the pictures they took with the cell phone. Some pictures showed the approaching storm and were dramatic. When the fiancé came up to us, I took their picture and gushed like a silly old woman. How romantic!

- *A woman's water broke and they were driving to Cherokee with the car emergency lights flashing. There was a lot of ranger discussion about where the car was and trying to find it so they could escort them out of the park. That seemed to take a long time and we never did hear them find the car. Rangers were reporting their locations and the lack of a car with the flashing lights all along US 441.*

A camper came to the motorhome just as we were getting ready to eat. A big ole red hound dog was following him. The man said the dog had been wandering around the campground all morning. They fed her some leftover sausages. He had asked everyone in the campground if the dog was theirs. She was friendly and didn't bother the children in the campground. She was definitely sniffing around, trying to find something. Andy began looking for a piece of rope to tie her up, but she took off down the horse trail and into the woods. I told the man there was no point in calling the park to come get her if we could not catch her. I did call dispatch to report the dog, just in case someone was looking for her. He said there were two missing-dog reports in the Cataloochee area over the mountain from us. We could hear her barking that deep hound dog bark way down in the woods.

The hound dog returned to the group site. I went over with a handful of rib meat Andy had saved in case she came back. The three little girls in the group site kept chasing the dog and she kept going farther away. I told the girls not to chase her because I wanted to catch her and return her to her owners. When they backed off, I was able to get closer to the dog. One chunk of rib meat and she was mine. She followed me back to our site where Andy was busy opening a package of rope and trying to unroll it. I parceled out the bits of meat slowly to give Andy time to make a leash before I ran out. He made a loop and we slipped it over her head while she was eating one of the last bits of rib. We ran the rope around her chest to make a halter and then Andy tied the rope to a tree. This was a delicate operation, as the dog must have had several litters of puppies in the past and had two rows of teats hanging down. She had some ticks and her left eye was irritated, but she did not feel too dirty. She was not terribly thin, so she must not have been out in the woods for long.

I had seen a dog truck drive through several times in the past few days, but this dog did not have a tracking collar. I called dispatch on the radio to report that we had caught the dog. He asked me to call him on the telephone, so I drove the car to a spot with a cell signal and called. Dispatch said he was going to forward the call to Ranger Chuck. This was my chance, "Wait, wait, first, the baby, tell me whether it was a boy or a girl." He chuckled and said the mother did get to the hospital in time, but they had not heard any news. He thought the child should be named Smoky, whatever the gender.

Then he forwarded me to Chuck who explained that hunting dogs were an issue. They are expensive dogs and their owners get riled up if they are taken to a shelter. When a dog is near the edge of the park, they generally do not do anything with it. If the dog is deep within the park, they will pick it up. If the dog has a tracking collar, they can get the phone number off it and call the owners to come get it. Getting the hint, I proposed that I take the dog down to the park entrance, one mile away, and let her go. He agreed by saying, "pat her on the fanny and send her on her way." He added that if she returned the next day, give him a call and he would come up with a plan. Andy pointed out that we could not get the dog into the car; she was too big and the car was too small. So we let her go at our campsite. She took off into the woods barking that incredibly loud and deep hound dog bark. We could hear her for a long while. Then four deer ran across the horse trail and up the hill.

Boss Larry came to see us at noon with a new box of payment envelopes and stayed for an hour or so. I offered Larry a cup of coffee and we chatted for a while, mostly about park matters and happenings. Then we got to the subject of the stolen pickup truck. Larry, a native of Gatlinburg, told us stealing vehicles and chopping them apart for parts is part of the Cocke County economy.

- *Apparently, a small child, referred to as a baby by the ranger, had been burned. The chest, shoulder, and back had second or third degree burns. The parents had decided not to wait for an ambulance, but to drive the child to the local hospital themselves. When the ranger reported the degree of the injury to dispatch, they decided to try to intercept the family car to get the child transported to Children's Hospital by helicopter. As with the woman in labor, rangers were reporting their locations and where along the route they would try to intercept. Later, a ranger reported that he had talked to an ambulance driver and the family was already at Blount Memorial Hospital in Maryville.*

- *Dispatch called for any available rangers to go to a motor vehicle accident at "the spur." An ambulance was on the way for an unresponsive patient. When the ranger got on the scene, he called dispatch and reported, with more than a bit of exasperation in his voice, "They're just out of gas!" The people who had run out of gas had no idea how they got reported as "unresponsive." Dispatch quipped, "It must have been the car that was unresponsive."*

- *A woman in the Greenbrier parking lot called the park emergency number to report a man there was about to burn the place down. I presumed that meant he had a huge campfire rather than that he was an arsonist, but it could go either way.*

When Daughter Kathy came for a Father's Day visit, we decided to share our newfound biscuit-making skills and served biscuits and country ham for breakfast. I made the biscuits larger than usual and each of us could only eat one. Chuck came to pick up pay envelopes. He accepted my offer of a country ham biscuit. I asked Chuck what happened with the burned child and he told us the child was a fifteen-month-old toddler who pulled a pot of boiling water off the camp stove. He suffered second-degree burns and was taken to the burn unit at Vanderbilt in Knoxville for treatment.

- *An older man fell in the barn in Cataloochee. A park volunteer called 700 for assistance. CPR was in progress by volunteers immediately, but there was no pulse. The son wanted them to continue the CPR anyway. There were frantic calls for a helicopter. It was awful to hear. We were sure the man had died as time passed, but the rescue people did not give up. The man was taken to a hospital, but did not survive. It is sad enough to have your dad drop dead of a heart attack any time, but on an outing to the park for Father's Day must be extra tough.*

The tent campground was littered with poison ivy leaf bits after Spence went through with the weed whacker. He joined us outside for coffee and talk just before noon. Some road crew guys came by in a truck. One got out, talked to Spence for a bit, and gave him a hard time about not listening to his park radio. Spence countered that he can't hear it when he is wearing ear protection and whacking weeds, mowing, or blowing leaves.

- *A park engineer was driving on the mountain road between Big Creek and Cataloochee and came upon a motorcycle accident. The motorcycle was down off the road, but the biker was lying on the shoulder under a tarp, as it was raining. At first, the people did not think the man was hurt. They must have used their cell phone to call for a tow truck, which was already on the scene. However, the tow truck could not reach the motorcycle with the injured man lying on the road in too much pain to move. The park engineer said they thought he might have some broken ribs. At one point, dispatch asked how long the man had been lying on the road and she answered about two hours. It was several more before he rode out in the ambulance.*

- *The bear sow with three cubs had returned to the Cade's Cove stables. She was chased off once, but returned an hour later. Wildlife people were on the way and I worried about what was to become of the mama and babies. I hope they were moved to a remote part of the park where the babies would not learn things that get them into trouble.*

- *Dispatch called for a ranger to help a park visitor by jump-starting the car. Another ranger responded that they were not supposed to use their cars for jump-starts because it messed up the ranger car's camera.*

Boss Larry showed up again in the afternoon. He came to our site and chatted for a while. It may not seem like a big deal, but Larry's visits were always a morale booster for us. He always made a point of how much the park needs and appreciates us. Then, he usually made some smart aleck quip when he left.

- *Two trucks pulling horse trailers had an accident at the loop, but it was not clear whether it was with another vehicle, a rock, or each other. They had traffic backed up in both directions. "The loop" is literally a loop, or spiral, in the road up on the steep mountainside. The discussions on this problem went on for hours. Apparently, one of the trucks needed a tow. Then there was discussion about the horse trailer he was towing. Would the horses be in the trailer while it was being towed? The horses must have been moved to the other horse trailer. The tow truck was going to tow the pickup and the horse trailer together. This incident must have created a massive traffic backup on the busy Newfound Gap Road.*

Boss Larry surprised us by showing up again the next day. He came over to fill a pothole in the parking lot. I am certain that filling potholes is not in Larry's job description. This is yet another example of how dedicated many park employees are.

- *There was a motorcycle accident on the Clingman's Dome road. The rider's arm was hurt and the driver had an abrasion on his left leg. They declined an ambulance, but the rangers were still stopping traffic in all directions to get the ambulance on the scene. The motorcycle was thirty yards down a steep slope.*

- *There was another bear incident. A female ranger said she was going to escort a woman back to her campsite to get her camping gear. A second person asked if she had bear spray and when the response was no, the female ranger was told not to go to the campsite. Some other bear specialists were going in to close the campsite and to retrieve the woman's gear. The camper did not have her car keys or driver's license with her so she was stuck there.*

- *A bear got into a tent at backcountry Campsite 18. Dispatch called for a wildlife unit to investigate.*
- *A park visitor took pictures of other visitors feeding a bear and of their license plate. Several rangers were on the lookout for the car. Those people could get a fine up to $5,000 and a jail sentence up to six months. I hoped the rangers caught them, but never heard. Feeding a bear is a death warrant for the bear, which had associated people with food and lost its fear of them.*
- *A bear was reported on Newfound Gap Road near the Sugarlands Visitor Center.*
- *A ranger was out with a bear at the Gap.*
- *A ranger reported they had the bear in a trap at the riding stables. Another one was out running around. That must have been the mama with three cubs we heard about earlier.*
- *A ranger was in a cemetery, on the radio with 700, and asked her to call what must have been a lost party on the phone and ask him if he could hear a whistle. He did not. Two rangers were going to hike up the trail and blow a whistle every fifteen minutes until the guy could hear it. Then, he was to call 700 again on his cell phone. They also were going to try calling the guy directly when they got a cell signal. At 8:10, dispatch reported to the rangers that the guy heard the whistle. He had called Wayne County Police, who called the Park. Then, we did not hear any more about it. We can only suppose the fellow followed the sound of the whistle and met up with the rangers on the trail. He had apparently wandered off the trail to see if he could find a view and then could not find the trail again. After reading "Lost! A Ranger's Journal of Search and Rescue" by Dwight McCarter and Ronald Schmidt, I decided that I would never, ever leave the established trail and wander off into the woods. At least, no more than a few feet to duck behind a bush for privacy.*

Andy went up to the campground while I got busy on the 78-10/12 birthday cake. Heath had subtly suggested Key Lime Cake. Culinary Disaster! The recipe calls for a box of lemon cake mix and a box of lemon instant pudding mix. I guess they don't make lime cake mix or lime pudding mix. (The lime flavoring comes from lime juice.) As I was pouring the pudding mix into the bowl with the cake mix, something was different. I checked the box and, sure enough, I had bought and poured in Lime Jell-O mix. I could not think of anything to do other than press on. It did occur to me to add another egg since eggs make pudding. In it went. The batter was an alarming shade of green.

Spence dropped in at quitting-time for a piece of monthly birthday cake. He had been using the Gator to empty ashes from the campground fire rings. First, he dumps a bucket of water in the ring to make sure there are no hot coals. Then he shovels the mush into the back of the Gator. Next, he drives the Gator to the horse campground and dumps the wet ashes into the trailer used for horse manure and hay when they clean out the stalls. When he was finished, he came to the motorhome, used our water hose to rinse out the back of the Gator, and then loaded it back onto the trailer.

I sliced three pieces of cake and we all joked about who was going to be the first one to take a bite and turn as green as the cake. Spence went first. "Ain't <u>nuthin'</u> wrong with that cake." Andy was the second. "Good Babe." I figured it was safe and took a bite. It was fine in spite of the atomic green color. Andy told Spence that when I yell "Culinary Disaster!" it is going to be good. Spence pointed out, "This was a Color-nary Disaster."

- *A yearling bear had been run over near the construction zone and appeared to be alive when the reporting party saw it. Later, the people who hit the cub stopped in the visitor center to report it. Park personnel went to investigate, but could not find the bear.*

- *In a traffic stop, the ranger gave a verbal warning for a child not restrained in a car seat. I would have given the maximum possible. What excuse could he possibly have to be that lenient?*

- *There was a group of people performing Baptisms by a bridge and it was causing traffic backups. I have to admit, if I saw that scene while driving on a mountain road, I would stop and take a picture.*

- *A ranger in the Cherokee area had a man handcuffed in the back of the ranger truck. The ranger was requesting help because there was a child in the back seat of the man's car.*

- *A ranger stopped a vehicle with four or five young people as well as booze and marijuana. Two of them were under eighteen. The ranger asked 700 to call the parents of the kids to get their permission for the underage kids to ride home with the adults and substances and gave her the parent's names and phone numbers to call. Dispatch called back a bit later to report that one of the "parents" was a girl who said she was a friend who had grown up with the boy. Oops, not the mom. That ploy didn't work.*

Andy built a fire and we sat outside for most of the evening. We heard Heath over in Cosby and both of us knew he was on his way to Big Creek. Heath was assisting some people who were locked out of their car. When he was clear of that, we looked at our watches and noted he would arrive in about half an hour. He showed up right on time. Always thoughtful, Heath was sure to observe Andy's monthly birthday. I went inside and sliced him a big piece of key lime cake.

Andy met a backpacker in the parking lot who had come back down off the trail for more food. Mice had gotten into his backpack and destroyed everything. And, everyone is so worried about the bears.

- *The Job Corps leader called for a ranger. One student had punched another. The students were separated; the puncher was in the administrative office and the punchee was with the nurse.*

- *A young male at Laurel Falls had a bad gash on his head and was losing blood. A ranger told the caller (a park volunteer) to put a t-shirt or something on the gash with pressure to control bleeding. Later, the reporting party said they had stopped the bleeding and the man was walking down the trail.*

- *About eighteen Harley motorcycles were traveling at a high rate of speed and passing illegally, heading toward "the tail of the dragon." That is a section of road near Deals Gap on the Tennessee/North Carolina border at the opposite end of the park. It has 318 sharp curves in eleven miles.*

- *A ranger called 700 to say he would be out with two coyote pups sitting beside the road.*

- *A park visitor called the park to say his wife was following him in another car with the three children. The wife apparently missed the turn and continued along the road. Dispatch described the car and announced to rangers in the area to stop the wife and direct her to the Elkmont Campground. Just a few minutes later, someone called 700 to say he had made contact with the wife. You probably don't get that kind of service from law enforcement outside of a national park.*

- *Park volunteer "Laurel Falls Rover" called 700 to report a woman in a motorized wheelchair had gone over the edge of the paved trail with three people. There were injuries. He sounded somewhat panicked and said, "Send help right away!" He repeated his call for help several times. He said she was not responding to questions, but was breathing. Then, "She said her name!" The wheelchair had gone off a rock wall near the falls and was about half way down. It turned out to be just the woman in the wheelchair who was injured. The other two had rushed down to help her. The first ranger to arrive called for more help. He said he needed four or five more people at the falls. Rescue One was in route. The ranger in charge told one person to close the trail when they got there. Another person was called to come on scene to cover the road. Then he told Laurel Falls Rover to clear all the people from the area. The woman had severe facial injuries. She weighed about 330 pounds and fell about twenty feet vertically down a gravelly surface. The ranger called for a technical rescue team. Other rangers and park personnel were chiming in to help. At 3:08, someone announced that the team had the woman back up and were heading down the trail, and for dispatch to call for Life Star again. Dispatch reported that Life Star was not available to fly. The litter was at the trailhead at 3:38. And, that is all we heard about that, except for conversations on clean up.*

- *The Greenbrier host called dispatch to say a fifteen-month-old child was locked in a running car. Chuck, who had been on his way to Laurel Falls, went to assist. A park VIP opened the car and rescued the toddler.*

- *The Elkmont campground host called 700 to report a camper was locked out of his car. Dispatch asked if he needed to go somewhere right away, but the host replied that the man was Asian and all he could understand was the man had no money. A ranger replied right away when 700 asked if anyone was available to help the man.*

I wondered if there are ever times when the rangers say, "Now I've seen it all." Then again, they probably know better than to say it. There is always something new happening in the park. That day was particularly eventful with two emergency rescues in progress at the same time, an arrest, and a toddler locked in a running car.

Every woman in the campground had told us about the toilet in the ladies room. Spence had been complaining about it too. It was something he could not fix. It is not in his job description and he does not have the parts. It needs a new doughnut seal. The water ran continuously. The toilet wobbled when sat upon. Moreover, it was filled with toilet paper and would not flush. I called dispatch to ask for someone who could fix it to come and do so. It was less than an hour later when we got a call on the radio from someone who was on the way over to fix it. It was Richard, Spence's team leader from Cosby. He was in the ladies room such a short time I thought his fix was to lock up the stall so no one could use it and hoped he at least turned off the water. Alas, I prejudged. He returned later with parts to fix the toilet. He said he could not fix the wobble, because the toilet was fastened to the floor with plastic fittings that keep breaking.

- *We thought we had heard just about everything there was to hear on the park radio, and then heard that someone left a loaded 9 mm Glock in a men's room. This was troubling that someone brought it into the park and left it loaded, in a restroom where a child could find it and hurt or kill themselves or someone else.*

- *I still had not heard it all. The next morning, someone called the park office to report a man in a wheelchair riding in the back of a pickup truck. He was apparently not secured well and the reporting party was concerned for his safety.*

Blueberries were on sale at Food City and I bought two boxes. They could not just sit in the fridge, so I made a cobbler. I had taken it out of the oven to cool. Then, we heard Heath on the radio telling someone he was near Big Creek. We laughed and said he has a great sense of smell. However, he did not stop in to say hello and missed a serving of warm cobbler. His sense of smell is not as good as we thought it was. When I told him about it later, he said I should have called for him on the radio. I didn't need to say cobbler; I could just ask him to stop by the host site.

Spence complained about a mess in the campground men's room. It was apparently so bad that he told Andy and not me. I suppose that is because he could not describe it without cussing, which he would not do in front of me. Andy relayed that it was all over the toilet and floor. Later in the afternoon, after he had cleaned it up, Spence theorized that someone had attempted to use the toilet while standing up and missed. Junior, in Site 8, told me the men's room was so bad that he walked down to use the toilet in the picnic area. As hard as he works picking up trash, mowing, and weed whacking, Spence is not paid enough for that.

Heath and Boss Larry came by a bit before 2:00 to get the money out of the iron ranger at the campground. I served them both some blueberry cobbler. When I told Heath it was my Grandma Dorothy's recipe, he said to thank her for passing it on. I told him Grandma Dorothy had been dead for years. He said, "Then I'll thank her myself when I get to heaven."

We had already started a campfire with the charcoal leftover from cooking, so Andy stayed to tend the fire and I took the evening campground walk. After checking the registration board, I stopped to chat with Junior in Site 8. He was a regular and an interesting camper personality. He came in early in the day and registered for a site. Then he put up a tarp and set out his chairs. I think he slept in the back of his pickup truck in the parking lot. He would stay around for a day or two and then decide to leave early. He would tell arriving campers that he had already paid for the site, but decided to go home, and they could have it.

- *The Cosby campground host called 700 to report that a camper had burned his hand on the grill and needed medical assistance. He had a piece of plastic, or something, attached to his hand. My stomach did a little flip when I heard that.*

- *A ranger chased a bear and three cubs from the area between the campground and stables at Cade's Cove. Mama and two cubs ran into the woods, but one cub was separated. The wildlife person he was talking to decided it would be OK. As long as the cub did not have to cross a road, it would find its mama again. The wildlife person asked if the mama had ear tags, but the ranger did not see any. That meant it was not the same mama and cubs they had caged a while back.*

- *Reservations are required for backcountry sites, but those sites still do not ensure solitude in the wilderness. One evening a backcountry hiker called the park on the phone to say the backcountry shelter on Mount Collins he had reserved had a "squatter" in it. The unkempt person had knick-knacks hanging all about the shelter. The caller was not comfortable staying there with the person occupying the site. Dispatch checked the records. The Mount Collins shelter accommodates eight campers. Three spots were reserved, but 700 could not tell whether the unkempt camper was one of them since the caller had not provided a name. If he was one of those with a reservation, he was perfectly legal, kempt or un. I spent the rest of the evening trying to visualize what kind of knick-knacks might have made the caller uncomfortable.*

A camper came to report that the men's room toilet had been trashed again. He was polite and said feces, which were all over the toilet and floor. The toilet was full of paper and unusable. It was Spence's day off, so I called Richard in Cosby on the radio twice, but he never answered. No one did. I decided to call park dispatch with the phone. We needed to run out to the grocery store, so I stopped the car by the river and called dispatch to report the toilet problem on the way out. He said people had taken off early for the holiday, but he would try to find someone to come clean it up.

Dispatch called us on the radio just as we were returning from the grocery store to say the Indiana man whose pickup truck had been stolen a few weeks before would be there in an hour or so to pick up his camping gear we had stowed in the ranger station.

Andy went in to check the status of the men's room during our campground walk. It had not been cleaned up. I called dispatch on the phone.

"This is Big Creek Host. I have a full campground here and the men don't have a toilet. There is poop on the toilet and on the floor. The toilet is full of toilet paper and can't be flushed. And, just for the record, this is the second time this has happened in three days!" There was a moment's pause.

"Would you say it's a mess?"

He stopped me mid-rant and I had to laugh. "Yes, I would say that."

He forwarded me to Paul, the head of maintenance, who was probably at home at that point. I repeated my tirade. He promised he would find someone to come clean it up or would come himself. He told me this happens once in a while. Well, it was more than once in a while at Big Creek lately.

We were chatting with the couple in Site 6 when the man from Indiana walked up. Andy left with him to unlock the ranger station and get his camping gear out, and helped him load it into his new-to-him pickup truck.

Then I walked to the horse camp to get a head count for the night. The motorhome Andy had sent to park in the horse day-use lot in the morning was sitting in Site 5. The people had a campfire going and dinner was cooking on the grill. I told them Andy had sent them to park in the day lot where people park with horse trailers, not in a campsite. The horse campground is by reservation only. Moreover, it is for horse camping only. They could not stay there. Campsite 5 was already reserved by someone else. The apologetic man asked if there was anything I could do to help them. I guessed it would be all right for them to use Site 6, which had not been reserved, but he would have to pay the horse camp rate of $50. He was happy to pay and gave me a check. We chatted for a bit and then I decided Andy might be back from the ranger station and headed back to the host site.

Andy was not back yet, but the people had arrived in the group site. There were only two guys. One was Ken whom we had met some weeks before. He had told us he would be back with a motorcycle group for the holiday weekend. He and a buddy were there, but none of the rest of the group showed up. He said they would be happy to let other campers share their six-tent site if we needed the room this weekend. He said Andy had been there and went on to the campground looking for me.

I headed back up to the tent campground to find Andy. A park pickup truck was parked in front of the toilet building so I went to check on the progress. It was Spence, who came in on his day off to clean up the toilet mess. He was just finishing up. He said Andy had gone to the horse camp looking for me. He drove me back to the motorhome, but Andy was not there. I decided to sit by the RV and wait for Andy to return. Spence was happy to have been called in on his day off; he was getting time-and-a-half for a few hours.

I told Spence about the motorhome in the horse camp and that I made them pay the horse camp rate of $50.

"Fifty dollars! You cheated him; the horse camp is $25 a night!" Oops. I said I would go back down there and set it straight.

I kept glancing down the trail looking for Andy so Spence decided he would drive to the horse camp and pick him up. He found Andy walking up the road where he had come from the ranger station. When he did not find me in the horse camp, he figured I had gone to the ranger station looking for him, so he went to find me there. Spence had a good laugh at the two of us wandering around and around Big Creek trying to find each other.

I told Andy about charging the people in the motorhome $50 and I needed to go back to the horse camp to fix it. He snapped, "Let him pay $50. The park needs it. He told me this morning they were only going to be here a few hours while they went to the Midnight Hole. I told him to park in the horse camp day-use parking area. He knew what he was doing, but he didn't get away with it." OK, $50 sounds about right.

It was a beautiful fourth of July holiday at Big Creek. The hikers and picnickers began flooding in early. When campers left, their sites were taken over within minutes. We had an interesting conversation with Tony in Site 10. He was camping and hiking for his health in a more immediate way than most of us. He had Parkinson's Disease. The doctors told him to get out and be as active as possible and this is how he was doing it. He had some difficulty talking and expressed his frustration at not being the man he used to be. He never could have imagined being older and in poor health when he was young and athletic. The past two years had been difficult, but since they changed him to a new medicine, he had improved dramatically. I admired his courage and tenacity.

We were surprised in the morning when we saw seven vacant campsites in the tent campground. So many people go to a lot of trouble to set up elaborate campsites for only one night. The road was lined with cars parked in every possible spot. They could not pull off the one-lane road because there are boulders there meant to keep people from parking. So, they just parked in the road.

- *Somewhere in the park, a short bald man in a white t-shirt was walking in the middle of the road yelling and cursing at visitors and banging on cars.*

We walked along the creek again and took one more look off the bridge when we saw a ranger vehicle parked in front of our gate. We knew it belonged to Heath since we had heard him on the radio saying, "the parking at Big Creek is out of control." He was down at the motorhome looking for us. We met up on the lawn and discussed the craziness that was Big Creek. Heath said he had been down at the entrance to the horse camp directing people to park there. He had driven up to the campground and had trouble maneuvering around to get back out with all the cars parked in the road. Heath decided we needed a new sign and should close the gate to the campground road on weekends. There was a sign saying "Campers Only," but the cars parked in front of it hid it.

There were eight vacancies in the tent campground Sunday morning and in the afternoon there were still seven. Cars were still pouring in filled with picnickers, hikers, and folks heading for the Midnight Hole. Cars were parked everywhere, as usual. As busy as the campground had been the past few weeks, it was surprising how empty it was on the holiday weekend. My theory was that everyone figured there would be no sites available and went elsewhere.

Two hikers came in to report that there were two large dogs running around loose at the Midnight Hole and one of them was a pit bull. I called in to 700 and he checked to see if 422 (Heath) heard the report. He responded that he was on the way over. I had another blueberry cobbler in the oven.

We saw a ranger vehicle in the campground parking lot and heard Heath on the radio. He had given citations to two dog owners at the Midnight Hole. Andy built a fire and we sat by it waiting for Ranger Heath to come before I served the cobbler.

On Monday, I rode with Heath to the tent campground to witness him emptying the money envelopes out of the iron ranger. It was another photo opportunity missed. The ranger has to squat down and put his hand through a hole at the bottom of the post to unlock the box so it can be pulled out the top of the post. He pulled out the moneybox and it had a HUGE brown spider on the bottom of it. Heath did a little jig to shake the spider off his hand and the spider jumped back to the bottom of the box. Then, Heath got a stick to shoo the spider away. It did not go easily, but eventually ran off in the direction of the registration board. I vowed not to leave my camera behind again and to look all around me when I am reading the tabs on the registration board to make sure that spider is not over my head. There was already one medium-sized spider up there.

- *A young man, about twenty, was digging holes at Nolan Divide off the Deep Creek Trail. I thought that was rather odd and Spence explained that he was probably poaching ginseng.*

- *Three-four-six called 347 and said, "I need you to bring one of those paintball guns up here. I've got a bear that won't leave." I wondered what color that bear would be wearing that night.*

We heard thunder from the approaching storm as we walked back to the motorhome. Andy proposed that we skip the horse campground since no one was scheduled to be there. Then he added, "Some dey win, some deluge."

- *A crew cab truck with a utility box in the back had run off the road and hit a tree. It was taking two tow trucks to pull it out. The ranger on scene said they had one tow truck on the road with a chain attached to the pickup to keep it from sliding down the mountain any farther. The incident apparently had traffic backed up for a long way and people were making U-turns to get out of the backup. There are no alternate routes in the park.*

- *A ranger had emergency traffic at the Townsend "Y." A woman was cutting herself with a knife and emailing photos to her husband. Apparently, the husband called the park. The ranger was calling for a supervisor. That was Jared and he was In Charge. He called for other units to head to the "Y" as well. Dispatch got an ambulance on the way. The first ranger saw a blue minivan with Kentucky plates. The woman in the van said she was fine. Blount County said the woman told them her husband was lying. They decided to "stand down," but one ranger was going to talk to the woman just in case her husband was not lying. Whether he was lying or not, there is something deeply sad in that story.*

The people in Site 10 left a cooler and a box of food out unattended. The woman from Site 12 came over and thanked us for taking it away when she saw us. She was incensed, "It endangers everyone else!" We put it in the bear locker. Yay; someone was happy we were hauling off food. Of course, it was not hers.

The first of the group-site campers arrived as we were finishing our dinner. We chatted with the woman and her son and gave them a park brochure and newsletter. It was a Boy Scout group and they were working on their cooking badges. Later an SUV came in pulling a trailer load of boxes, furniture, and coolers.

- *Someone left a dog in the car at the Deep Creek trailhead parking lot. It had been there several hours. Later, the county police opened the car and gave him some water. The owners returned and the officer gave them a ticket.*
- *Wildlife people were tracking a bear near Cherokee Orchard. One fellow spotted it and said it matched the description perfectly, but not the behavior. Maybe it was a problem bear being good at the moment. The bear had a dark brown snout and a white spot on its chest. The man took pictures and sent them to the office. They discussed the bear for a while and then the one on the scene darted the bear and it was "down for the count." Later, they decided it was not the bear they were looking for.*

One of the fathers from the Boy Scouts in the group site passed us on our way up to the campground in the morning. I asked him how it was going.

"Great! The boys are doing a good job and making great food. I am eating well." To earn their merit badge, the boys had to plan the meals, do the shopping, gather the equipment, cook the meals, serve, and clean up. He thought the Boy Scout cooking merit badge was the best thing ever.

- *A white Honda Civic with California plates was driving through the park. The occupants had broken into another vehicle at Newfound Gap and stolen a purse. Several rangers were in pursuit while the victim was waiting at Newfound Gap. Witnesses said the robbers were two females. A ranger spotted a Challenger with California tags, but it had male and female occupants. Dispatch was on the phone with the victim and relaying information to the rangers on the road. She reported the white car would be followed by a black pickup with a male. Someone had reported hearing the male ask the females, "Did you get it?" We heard one ranger report a sighting. Dispatch called Gatlinburg to ask a unit to help. They planned to pull the Honda over at the Park Headquarters and the pickup at Sugarlands Riding Stables entrance. Dispatch looked up the tags and reported that the owner was Jesse James Xxxxx. We could not help laughing and even thought we heard 700 giggle. Then we heard "Two detained." Another tag was called in. We heard Heath say they may not have the right pickup. The one he pulled over had Georgia plates with two adults and small children in it. They decided to release the black pickup.*

Two of the girls in Site 4 looked as though they were leaving the campground. Andy called to them to be sure not to leave any food out. They said they had not and took off in a hurry. We walked by and noticed food and wrappers. I unzipped the screen room to get dirty trash off the table and found a grocery bag with peaches in it. I tossed in other assorted food items and put it in the bear locker. Andy took the trash to the dumpster. I hate it when they lie.

10

National Park Employees

The national park system means many things to Americans. It's the preservation of the feel of grandeur of the lands that make up our great nation. The national parks are America's playground. For millions. A quick Google search told me that in 2015, there were over 305 million visitors. That's a lot of people — and all their attendant waste — to handle.

While I have always loved my national park experience—the camping, hiking, the "getting away" from everyday life—when I volunteered, I realized that national parks are about community as much as anything else.

There is a wonderful group of people who make the park experience consistent year in and out for all those millions of people. Most aren't aware of the network of employees any one national park needs to keep it working. And, after spending summers volunteering, I can safely say, none of them classify as bureaucratic waste.

When most people think of national parks, I bet the first employee they think about is the park ranger. There are not many jobs that have quite the aura of romance or immediate recognition as they do with their olive pants, grey shirt, that flat top hat, and the National Park Service emblem on their sleeves. I love the rangers I work closely with. However, it didn't take me long to realize that the national parks employ a wide range of workers to keep things running smoothly. I asked the park's Public Information Office about it. Of course, the numbers and mix of employees changes continually, so here is a snapshot:

In July, 2014, there were roughly 336 people employed at the Great Smoky Mountains National Park. These folks worked full-time, part-time, or seasonally, and were either permanent, term, or seasonal employees. Each division of the park divides their staff up according to the needs and responsibilities of the division. It might just be a laundry list, but like Thoreau chronicled how much nails cost in Walden, I'm going to give you the run down on who works where. Thoreau's nails were supposed to symbolize thrift. The same could be said for the scant number of people working to make the 816 square miles of the Great Smoky National Park work efficiently—every day of the year:

Management Division: 5
Administration Division: 9
Resource Education Division: 30
Resource and Visitor Protection Division: 66
Facilities Management Division: 168
Resource Management and Science Division: 43
Wildland Fire Cache: 15

These numbers seemed like a lot of employees to manage wilderness until I did a bit more digging and found out what these divisions do. Management and administration doesn't seem too big for the size of the organization; they are certainly not top heavy. They and the fire department seem self-explanatory, so I'll just concentrate on the others.

Resource Education Division: 30 employees

These are the people who educate park visitors. Their methods include ranger-led nature walks, museums, visitor centers, brochures and guides, the park web site, and wayside exhibits. Their goal is to provide the visitors with an understanding and appreciation of the park and its resources and to inspire them to protect it. In 2015, the park reported nearly eleven million visitors to the park. Thirty people working to educate that many people is hardly a lot.

Resource and Visitor Protection Division: 66 employees

These are the law enforcement park rangers. They are primarily engaged in enforcement of federal and state laws and regulations against criminal threats to park resources and visitors; public safety, involving search and rescue and emergency medical services; management of front country campgrounds and backcountry use; wildland fire suppression; and response to roadway accidents. Given all the experiences I've shared about people breaking park *rules, getting in accidents, and not behaving like responsible park visitors—it's amazing that sixty-six men and women can keep as much order as they do.*

Facilities Management Division: 168 employees

This must be the toughest job in the park, with none of the glamour and admiration showered on the rangers. They also perform their job with an insufficient budget, which requires careful monitoring of conditions and prioritizing maintenance and repairs. They are responsible for roads, including sixty bridges, fallen trees, snow and ice, and potholes. They maintain 124 park buildings, including forty-six houses for park employees, ten campgrounds, nine picnic areas, twenty-seven water and wastewater systems, eight hundred miles of trails, sixty trail bridges, and 150 cemeteries with more than fourteen-hundred grave sites. These are also the folks who get to handle the outhouses. Enough said.

Resource Management and Science Division: 43 employees

This division's goals are to keep the wilderness wild, maintain the historical-cultural landscapes and buildings, monitor and control invasive species, monitor and protect endangered and protected species of plants and animals, control invasive animals and insects, monitor air quality, monitor water quality in the park's twenty-one-hundred miles of streams and rivers, protect the park's museum collections, maintain archeological sites, and inventory natural resources including soil and vegetation. They also attempt to herd bears and elk. It's a constant battle. Human bodies are hard on ecosystems, especially those who don't pay attention or are unfamiliar with the best practices when it comes to leaving a minimal impact on a wilderness area. So these forty-three employees are never idle.

About eighty of the park employees are seasonal and work in Resource Management & Science, Resource Education, Maintenance, and Resource & Visitor Protection.

It is important to remember the park also has over three thousand volunteers to help support its mission. Just because we work for nothing doesn't mean we are not a significant resource for the park. The volunteer page on the web site says, "Explore, learn, and share your time and talent while helping us protect this special place! From assisting with cultural demonstrations and special events, to adopting a trail or campsite, to serving as campground hosts, to helping fisheries biologists monitor trout populations... and everything in between, the work our volunteers do makes a difference! We have a variety of volunteer opportunities for individuals and groups, including many that do not require training."

I downloaded the volunteer list of identified needs for 2015. Volunteers work on trail rehabilitation projects. They adopt a trail and monitor and report trail conditions, blowdowns, hazards, and provide information to hikers. They adopt and maintain vistas by removing litter and trimming vegetation to keep the view open. They pick up litter along roads. They sow and transplant seedlings for restoration and revegetation projects. Those with prior law-enforcement experience patrol roads to assist visitors, help with traffic control, give minor roadside assistance, and assist with traffic control associated with wildlife viewing. Some can perform data entry and edit reports at home. The park needed a bicycle patrol person in Cataloochee. Laurel Falls and Rainbow Falls trails use rovers to monitor the visitors and call a ranger when the inevitable injuries and bear problems occur. Volunteers interview anglers to gather data on fishing in the park. And the list goes on. And on.

These are the people that make up the foundational community of a national park, and my hat is off to all the work they do. I am honored and humbled to do my small part.

But community can only be made up of individuals, and while you have met these characters already, I want to mention four who hold a special place in my heart.

First, there are two rangers. To put it succinctly and in my opinion, park rangers are the grown-up version of boy (and girl) scouts. They migrate to this job because they love the outdoors. They get the job because they beat out all the fierce competition for these coveted positions. They want to do good deeds. Park rangers are well trained and in great physical condition. Just like firefighters and police, they risk life and limb to protect the park visitors. OK, I confess, I fell in love with every one of them. They are just so adorable!

Ranger Tim Rand, and then Ranger Heath Soehn, are the two we knew best because they visited Big Creek the most. Both of them almost always stopped by to check on us and express their appreciation for our efforts. Then, beyond mere professional courtesy, they befriended us. Ranger Tim moved on to other parks and had a definite career plan. I have no doubt that he is well on the way toward his career goals. Ranger Heath, a native of Gatlinburg, is more interested in staying in the Smokies and interacting with park visitors on the front lines. You don't have to talk to him for long to understand why we called him Rescue Ranger Heath (I also call him Dudley Do-right, for those who remember the Rocky and Bullwinkle show); he seemed to always be out there saving hikers in distress.

I have already talked about the maintenance personnel, but they bear mentioning again. Without the maintenance department, the more than ten million visitors would turn the pristine wilderness and well-groomed front-country facilities into a disaster area in short order. I bet a park without the maintenance staff could be the basis for a disaster horror movie.

There is one maintenance man you've already met that towers above the others in my experience. Robert Spence. He is a cleaning, mowing, weed-whacking whirlwind. (I bet you never thought a national park needed weed-whacking, but the place would be uninhabitable without it). He likes to chastise me when I take a picture of him working. Says it would ruin his reputation. Then, he complains if I take a picture of him taking a break. I am sure there are others who work in the park who are just as proud of their area of responsibility as Spence is of Big Creek.

Boss Larry likes to give Spence a hard time about how much effort he puts into pretending to work. But you only have to take a look around Big Creek to know someone has been working hard to keep it in tip-top shape. All the regular campers know it and so do we campground hosts. His team leader, Richard, told me he knows he can always depend on Spence to do what needs to be done and to do a good job. We did meet the maintenance workers from Cosby when they would come over to clean the restrooms on Spence's days off. It was usually Linda, who was very conscientious about her job too. Spence says she does a better job on the restrooms than he does.

Our Boss Larry is a Visitor Use Assistant. He is responsible for collecting and accounting for campground fees, answering visitor questions, and providing them with park information. Since he covers a number of campgrounds, he provides the park materials for us to hand out. He also makes sure that we have everything we need to perform our camp host job, including fresh batteries for the park radios. He also lets us know how much he appreciates our efforts. I call it the care and feeding of campground hosts. Larry thinks that's highly appropriate.

I looked on line for some Visitor Use Assistant job announcements to find out what Larry is supposed to be doing. It is telling that the last sentence in the duties section was, "Stressful situations may occur on a daily basis." I'm sure that refers to dealing with park visitors, not us delightful campground hosts.

Actually, I think it refers to the work each and every one of the Great Smoky National Park employees have to face. It takes a lot of work to make a national park seem wild, untouched. But the reality is, national parks are the most popular camping spots in America, and it takes a lot of people to make sure that you have the best, safest experience possible. So next time you see a park employee, thank them. If you have chocolate, give them a little present. It may make their day, and they certainly deserve it.

The old red hound dog came walking up to the campground. She looked considerably thinner than she was when we saw her a few weeks before. The little girls from Site 12 ran out to pet and hug the dog. Their mother and I both called to them at the same time not to hug a strange dog.

A number of cars were coming up the campground road as we were leaving. There was not enough room for the big pickup trucks to turn around without backing and filling several times. More cars arrived. There was not enough room for cars to pass in opposite directions because of the cars parked on the sides of the narrow road. It was gridlock on the campground road. Again.

We walked on down the road between the cars. Spence stopped his truck at the lower parking lot and was blocking the road with it to keep any more people from driving up to the campground. No one could come out either, but that didn't matter because they were all stuck facing uphill. The three of us stood at the intersection of the parking lot and campground road while Andy told drivers to park in the horse campground day-use lot.

Spence inspected the split-rail fencing that had been knocked down by cars parked along the curve. Again. I marveled at Spence's equanimity when the split-rail fence was repeatedly knocked down. He didn't cuss or say bad things about the park visitors; he just put the rails back up. And, this is a man with a bad temper.

Spence was planning to mow the grass around the ranger station. He looked at our moss lawn and said it might need trimming in a week or two. Andy and I both laughed at him and teased him about keeping the forest trimmed. The moss was perhaps an inch tall with a few leaves of grass sticking up here and there. Later, when we walked toward the campground, I was admiring our mossy lawn. It is nicer than grass; however, you probably have to live in a wet forest to have one.

The red hound dog was still around. She ran up the horse trail past our site and then back and forth several more times. She seemed to be on a mission. Silly me, I thought she was tracking bears or deer.

It was just before 5:00 when the rain stopped so Andy suggested that we walk around the tent campground before it started up again. As we walked to the parking lot, we could see the husky belonging to the people at the group picnic table humping the red hound dog. The husky was on a leash and his owner was pulling him away as hard as she could. The hound dog kept following him. I don't blame her; he was a handsome dog. All the adults and children at the group picnic table were yelling, screaming, and squealing. It was chaos. The woman led her dog into the woods and the hound dog followed.

Then, the woman came up to us and asked us to do something about that dog. I explained that she had been around several times. We caught her once and the park rangers said to let her go. I reported her again yesterday, but no one did anything. I also said there was not much they could do. By the time a ranger got there, the dog would be off in the woods chasing deer and turkeys. I assured the woman the dog was not a stray, but lived down the hill near the entrance to the park. The woman was upset the dogs were "doing it" in front of the children. I personally didn't see any harm in that, but did not argue the point. I still wonder how many puppies resulted from that dalliance.

The campground was misty with the sun shining through the trees. I paused for a few pictures of the creek along the way. The mossy rocks on the far side of the creek were brilliant in the sunshine.

Heath stopped by in the evening, just as I was pulling cocktail-rye bread topped with Swiss cheese out of the oven. How did he know? He had come over to get the pictures I had taken of the parking situation. He brought a memory stick, but I already had the pictures on a CD. He looked them over and was pleased with my work. He also enjoyed the melted Swiss on rye.

The next morning Spence and Andy went down to the horse camp to figure out how many parking spaces could be added near the day-use parking area. I headed up to the campground to walk around, thinking about parking spaces. Spence had told us that the number of parking spaces in Big Creek matched the capacity of the toilet buildings (and sewer system). So it would make sense not to add spaces unless they also added toilets. Yet, we also don't want to turn Big Creek into a large parking lot. It is supposed to be a natural area. Maybe, there should be a gate to limit the number of park visitors at a time. That would sure make the experience of swimming in the Midnight Hole closer to what people must go there for rather than the crowds encountered there. But having a gate would require employees to man it. The answer was beyond me.

- *A wildlife guy reported dealing with seven bears. Seven bears! They could make a quick meal of him if they wanted to.*

- *The campground host reported that a person was "on the ground" in the Elkmont campground. The man was 46 years old. The family said this had happened before, but had not decided whether they needed an ambulance.*

We were on the way to the horse camp when we noticed the Boy Scouts cutting down small trees and branches. Andy yelled to them to stop destroying the vegetation. I added they could only cut dead and down trees. When they saw us coming back from the horse camp, they hunkered down in the little hollow where they were working. Andy went to the group site and told one of the leaders to stop them from cutting down live wood. Just about every time Boy Scouts camped in the group site, they tore off into the woods with hatchets and chopped away.

That night, a distraught man knocked on the door around 8:00. It was still raining. He had a service dog and a crutch and said he was a vet trying to build up his strength and get his head together after being shot in the middle east. He had paid for and was going to a backcountry site that was closed due to bear activity. A park ranger told him to come here. He had gone to the full campground and a woman told him he should come talk to us. His degree of agitation, nearing hysteria, worried and frightened me. He did not have a tent or backpack. He said he travels military style. I told him to camp in our site for the night.

It rained all night. One of the Boy Scout leaders came over in the morning and told us they had offered a spare tent to the man and he stayed in it in the group site. Later, we met the wounded soldier in the parking lot. He was getting ready to hit the Big Creek trail. His service dog, Copper, was standing patiently by. The man's name is Richard and he had an ambitious hike planned, staying a night in Campsite 37 and another in Campsite 38. I realized how distressed he had been the previous night when I heard him speaking calmly and coherently in the morning. I asked what the dog does for him. He uses the dog's harness for balance. If he passes out, the dog wakes him up. When Richard dropped his hiking stick, Copper picked it up by the little ball attached to the top and gave it back to him.

I was angry when I found graffiti on my bridge! I told Spence about it and he had some choice words for the culprit. I planned to scrub it off the next day if Spence did not do it first.

- *Someone called dispatch to ask about people tubing at Deep Creek. He thought the water was too high, but could not find any regulations against tubing in high water. Someone else responded that park policy is to warn them, but not stop them. Then, Blount County called the park and asked for a ranger to visit the tube rental companies and tell them to stop renting out tubes and putting people in the water.*

- *A 911 call came in. Dispatch had GPS coordinates and a cell phone number, but no indication of what the emergency was. They called in Heath on his day off to respond to that. While he was headed there, 700 called him to say a vehicle had run into the ditch at Greenbrier. No one was hurt, but the reporting party said the driver appeared to be intoxicated. Devin was taken from the Hen Wallow rescue to help Heath with the intoxicated driver. Heath called in to say he had the intoxicated woman in custody and was taking her to Sevierville to get an alcohol test. Devin stayed to supervise Carr's wrecker to get her car back up the embankment. A bit later, Heath called in to report that the woman said she was sick and wanted to be taken to the hospital. When I asked him about it later, Heath told me that asking to go to the hospital is a common ploy by people hoping to avoid going to jail. She was very drunk. He didn't sound too sympathetic toward her.*

- *A car ran off the road between Metcalf Bottoms and The Sinks. The air bag had deployed. They announced emergency traffic only on the radio. A ranger said the car was not in the water as trees had stopped it. They closed Little River Road to traffic to retrieve the car.*

- *A ranger reported that two kayakers left from the Chimneys Picnic Area and headed down the river. Dispatch asked if they were geared up for it. He said to advise them not to go and, if that didn't work, it was good enough. Yeah, this is America and people are free to kill themselves doing something reckless if they want to! Andy's theory is that people might take more risks than normal in a national park because there are rangers to come rescue them.*

The Boy Scouts left. Andy spotted something in the group site so we walked over to inspect. It turned out to be a log the Boy Scouts had chopped to smithereens on one end. Chips and splinters covered the ground for a yard around the end of the log. Andy shrugged and said, "We told them they could cut things dead and down."

In the earliest years of the park's existence, visitors invaded the park and made a huge mark on the landscape with their camps. Campgrounds were established to keep the human impact contained in specific areas. I thought back to the first time I went to a campground in a state park and how shocked I was that the campsites were right next to each other. That wasn't camping out in the woods; there were too many other people around. But, after a few seasons in Big Creek, I began to see the wisdom in attempting to control the impact on the land. The campground itself shows signs of thousands of feet, and hands with saws and axes, destroying the natural forest. There is also the campground aura showing signs of humans trespass: the well-trodden path along the creek, the shortcut path from the toilet building up to the Big Creek Trail, and the myriad small paths through the forest made by firewood foragers. The human impact in Big Creek is much less than over in the Cade's Cove campground, where the whole forest floor along the creek has been trampled to dirt. Will the trampled area continue widening over the years until there are no trees or understory near the campground?

The next morning, I got the dishpan and a rag and gathered some cleaning supplies to get that graffiti off the bridge. My first choice was fingernail polish remover. Second, was some spray citrus oil. I got an SOS pad and a scrub brush from under the kitchen sink and headed to the bridge. Spence was up on the road above the parking lot rebuilding the split rail fence that had been knocked down yet again. It baffles me. It is a one-way road with no room to park. There is no reason for anyone to get close enough to the fence to knock it down. It still happens regularly. Spence complained bitterly; there he was working and I did not have my camera to take his picture.

I soaked two-fingertip's worth of rag with fingernail polish remover and rubbed the writing on the bridge. I had to rub hard and use half a bottle of polish remover, but it did come off, mostly. When I was done, I could still tell someone had written something and could see faint letters. I sprayed my citrus oil on it and wiped. It did not have much effect. I picked up the dry SOS pad and scrubbed the railing hard. The ghost of the writing disappeared. There was a smooth spot on the side of the bridge where I had scrubbed. I was not thinking kindly of the person who wrote on the side of the bridge while I assessed the damage to my fingernails.

It was an exceptional day, especially for Andy, when one of his work associates, Doug Bruder, and his wife Linda stopped in for a visit. They were on vacation and exploring the region. I had never met them, but remembered how highly Andy spoke of Doug when they were working together. "He's a brilliant kid. He'll do well." He was not a kid anymore and he had done well.

Doug and Linda wanted to see the famous Midnight Hole and Andy surprised me by saying he wanted to walk up there too. His knee had been bothering him when he walked up and down hills. Of course, he wanted as much time with Doug as he could get. It started to get a bit misty, but we never really got any rain. Eventually, Linda and I were walking ahead and getting to know each other while Andy and Doug were behind talking about old times and people they both knew.

It was the quietest day we had seen at Big Creek. The weather was dreary and it was a Monday. Only a woman and her daughter from Site 9 were at the Midnight Hole. The woman was sitting on a rock and watching her daughter climbing the boulders and jumping into the creek. We climbed down the bank to the water's edge. Doug and Linda wanted a better look at the waterfall so they took off their shoes and waded out into the stream. The Smokies waterfall book says the waterfalls are eight feet high. The boulders are fifteen feet high and the water is fifteen feet deep.

Our next stop was Mouse Creek Falls. There was plenty of water, due to recent rains, and the falls were gorgeous. This is another spot you just cannot capture with a camera. There are several small streams at the top that form the top portion of the falls, then a small pool part way down, before the water falls over a ledge and into the creek. Once down to Big Creek, Mouse Creek seems to turn and make another fall before blending in.

At night, I told Andy to remind me to make the monthly birthday cake in the morning. Then I decided to write myself a note. I wrote, "Make Cake." That was not good enough for Andy. He wanted the note to say, "Make Delicious Cake." I wrote "Delicious" at the bottom of the note and drew an arrow to the insertion point. Then I taped it to the microwave door. I think delicious is a synonym for chocolate in Andy's thesaurus.

I started making dinner as soon as the cake came out of the oven. Spence stopped in and ate his lunch, but left when we sat down to eat ours. I fixed spaghetti for dinner with one of the many containers of frozen sauce I had in the freezer. Andy would be happy to eat it every day. It was special because it was his 77-11/12 birthday. I gave him some extra parmesan and pine nuts on top. We were finishing our spaghetti when we heard Heath on the radio reporting an elk with a calf on the I-40 exit ramp at Waterville. We laughed at his timing and I went inside to frost the cake. A few minutes later, I saw Boss Larry walk up. He had come with Heath to empty the iron ranger at the tent campground – and to eat a piece of cake. I brewed a pot of coffee to go with it and we all enjoyed Fudgy Chocolate Layer Cake.

Sally and two girlfriends in Site 10 came down to the motorhome to have some of Andy's cake. Spence had finished his work for the day and stopped by to say good-bye as he did most days. He said he had been told that park employees should not be seen in uniform on their way home from work, in a convenience store buying cigarettes, beer, and lottery tickets. He had taken off his uniform shirt and put on a t-shirt. He shocked and amazed the women by taking the ties out of his pigtail and shaking his long hair loose. He was ready for cigarettes, beer, and maybe a winning lottery ticket.

- *A Clingman's Dome volunteer called 700 to say a man was walking down the Andrew's Bald Trail with a rifle. Apparently this upset a number of park visitors and they were all asking what was going on. Someone else came on the radio to say it was a park employee, a wildlife specialist, but did not say why he was carrying a rifle. A few hours later, someone else called 700 to say people were coming off the trail were reporting a man with a rifle.*

Having read "A Bear in the Back Seat" by Kim DeLozier and Carolyn Jourdan, I thought he must have been out to shoot some boar. Non-natives, they were introduced in a private hunting reserve in North Carolina in 1912 and have since spread throughout the park and into Tennessee. Now they are wreaking havoc by eating the endangered wildflowers, tearing up the forest floor near streams, eating the local wildlife such as the famous salamanders, and eating the food supply (notably acorns) of native species. Boars are also tearing up the forest floor near trails. Several times hikers had come off the trail and complained of the terrible destruction caused by the boars. The good news is that coyote, also making a comeback, are eating baby boars and helping to stem the population growth.

The next Boy Scout group had arrived when we got home from the grocery store. There were four men and sixteen boys. I gave them a Smokies Guide newspaper and a park brochure, answered questions and started the bear lecture. The man waved his hand and said they did not need the bear lecture. They did not have any food. This was going to be a fun weekend and they were not cooking. They were going to eat out! I described the local eateries, which meant fast food at the Newport interstate exit, and wondered what merit badge that would earn them.

As we walked through the day-use parking lot, we saw Heath drive in and stop at the closed campground road. He watched some campers come out of the gate and close it behind them. Then he pulled around into the parking lot and stopped by a family getting ready to leave. He waved to a small boy, turned on the flashing lights and siren, and then said, "Step away from the car!" through the loudspeaker. The little boy was in awe. Andy opened the gate to our site so Heath could drive in and help us finish off the 77-11/12 birthday cake.

- *A park visitor dropped his or her car keys into the pit toilet at Clingman's Dome. They were five feet down, on top of the pile. The Clingman's Dome volunteer said they got them out with a coat hanger. I hope he just gave the coat hanger to the key dropper and let them get their own keys off the pile. The volunteer said, "there is something new every day." Andy noted that if someone tried to kill himself in a pit toilet, it would be "sewercide."*

Boss Larry arrived just as we were finishing our meal. He came to say good-bye and thank us for volunteering. We talked about the parking situation. He said he had taken pictures of all the cars in the horse camp. I did say, as much as I loved being there, after three months, I was ready to move on. I was just about ready to start slapping people and I wanted to visit my family. We promised to return the next May and June.

Andy spoke with a woman who was driving the wrong way in the one-way parking lot. He told her to go park at the horse camp. Later, he saw her again parking along the road by the campground gate. She told Andy the horse day lot was full so she came back to the parking lot. Andy walked down to check on the horse camp and it was only half full. She had lied to him.

- *There was discussion all through the day between what seemed to be wildlife units. Their call numbers were 351, 358, 357, etc. Early in the day one was asking the other if they heard from "27" yet and could they listen for "32" next. At 6:15, one person asked another if they had any luck with the trap, but the second person had not reached it yet.*

The day before we were due to leave, we did not turn on the park radios. We did not care where people parked their cars. We walked around the campground that was nearly empty.

I invited Spence to eat lunch with us and finish up the chili. He helped Andy prepare for leaving. Spence used his leaf blower to get the debris out of the top of the slides on the motorhome. We moved the motorhome forward two feet to make sure it would move. I laundered our uniform shirts and fleece jackets. Then I packed up all the park materials I had spread out on the motorhome dash for the past three months. We took the park radios and the rest of it to the ranger station in the afternoon. We also left our set of keys on the desk and locked the door on the way out. On our last night in Big Creek, Andy and I sat by the fire until the rain drove us inside.

11

Another Season

The next May, I pulled back into the parking area by the Pigeon River. Andy disconnected the car from the motorhome while I called the Great Smoky Mountains National Park dispatch office on the telephone to let them know we had arrived. Spence was just getting ready to mow the grass at the ranger station. When he saw us, he came out to direct me across the one-lane bridge over Chestnut Branch. I didn't think I could do it without someone directing me as the narrow bridge is on a curve and there is a huge boulder right where I would want to swing wide to line up. Spence was standing too close to the front of the motorhome and I could not see him waving his arms to direct me. I just held my place. Eventually, Spence came around to the driver's window to see why I wasn't doing what he directed me to do. I opened the window, "I can't see you!" I didn't yell, but he told everyone for the rest of our stay how I yelled at him while he was trying to help me cross the bridge. The more I protested, the more he liked to tell, and embellish, the story.

We never met another vehicle coming down the road. I pulled up in front of our host campsite and waited for Andy to direct me to back in. The green emanating from the leaves, grass and under-story vegetation was powerful, almost tinging the air a pale shade of green. The leaves were not fully out, so we would have some sunshine if it came out from behind the clouds.

Spence stopped in to welcome us back when he finished working. A year had passed since his father died and left Spence the farm. Now, the sisters were taking him to court for some cash from the estate, which had no cash. He said the court date was in June. I had hoped the family feud would be over by then.

The sun was in and out behind small clouds for the morning walk. The leaves were wet from an early rain. It was brilliant. There was no sun as we walked up the road to the tent campground. Yellow Trilliums were everywhere and Big Creek was a torrent. There were a bazillion small brown grasshoppers everywhere. That is no exaggeration; it's an estimate. When we walked by them in the forest, their jumping in the dry leaves sounded like rain. We had not seen them in Big Creek before, but the forest was alive with them then. I mean grasshoppers in Biblical proportions.

- *Someone at Clingman's Dome reported that it was snowing up there.*

- *The snow was starting to stick. The park closed the road. There was ½ to ¾ of an inch at that point. A ranger called in tags for two cars parked there to see if they belonged to backpackers. Dispatch checked and both cars belonged to people who had registered for backcountry campsites for the night so they didn't have to worry about them driving out in the snow.*

Andy reported that the temperature was 47 degrees when he got up in the morning. It had warmed up to 48 by the time I was up. It started raining at 2:00 and rained lightly for the rest of the day.

- *A ranger saw a car driving very fast and passing on the winding mountain road, but he could not go after him because he was giving a ticket to a guy who was doing 65 in a 35 mile per hour zone. About eight minutes later another ranger pulled the driver over for speeding - again.*

- *Several road crew people were talking about putting "ice melt" on the roads and sidewalks at Clingman's Dome. Then, they decided it was safe to open the road.*

- *One-One-Eight said he was in the Greenbrier area and could hear a lot of gun fire. He knew he was near the park perimeter, but could not determine whether the gun fire was in the park or not. Dispatch called 422, Heath, to check it out. Sometime later, we heard Heath report back that the gunfire was a church group having target practice outside the park.*

Boss Larry stopped in to greet us and asked if we needed anything. He and his wife Kristen had taken a month-long trip to Australia and New Zealand over the winter. When he was a marine in Cambodia, he was scheduled to go to Australia for R&R, but they sent him back to the U.S. instead. He told the sergeant that he didn't want to go home; he wanted to go to Australia. Forty-five years later, he finally did it. His Uncle Sam did not pay for it though.

Richard came over from Cosby to check Big Creek on Spence's day off. He stopped to chat with us for a few minutes. We talked about the improvements that he and Spence had made since the previous year. Big Creek was looking good. Richard said he had worked in the park for sixteen years and had never seen the likes of those little brown grasshoppers. He wasn't exaggerating either when he said there were zillions of them.

Heath and Boss Larry showed up to empty the pay envelopes out of the iron ranger. Andy served them cookies. Then they sampled the biscuits. Heath asked me if they were hard to make "or can any fool do it?" I assured him that any fool can; Andy did.

I told Heath I had made the cookies for him since he would have to wait three weeks for Andy's monthly birthday cake. He said he had cake last week for his own birthday. He had turned 48. His oldest son was graduating from high school that month. Heath also announced that his wife Dana, the park's Public Information Officer, had been named Park Employee of the Year a few days before.

After eating cookies and biscuits, Heath told Larry that he needed a nap and Larry would have to drive his ranger truck back to Cosby. Larry asked if he could flash the lights and sound the siren. Then, he told of a time when he was riding with Ranger Jared and tried to talk on the park radio. He was calling dispatch, who did not respond to his call. Then, Jared noticed that Larry was using the microphone for the exterior megaphone and not the park radio. When they left, Heath was driving and said good-bye to us with the megaphone.

- *A car had been broken into and a purse was stolen. A park ranger told dispatch to have the victim bring the car to the ranger station so he could see the damage and determine whether it was a theft or simply a loss.*

Spence and Linda dropped by after they finished cleaning the toilet buildings. It was Linda's first day back at work for the season. Her work year is about six months long. Spence had come back earlier than most seasonal workers because he did some other maintenance work around the park. I listened to Spence and Linda talk about being unemployed for half the year. Some people get unemployment checks, but apparently some do not. Spence mentioned a woman who didn't get her unemployment checks until she was already back at work the next season. Linda told me that it is very difficult to get a year-round, full-time job in the area. Employers do not want to pay any benefits, especially health care.

Drats! The microwave/convection oven seemed to be dying. It would only run for about fifty seconds before shutting down. That explained the flat cookies I had made the day before.

Spence told us that he almost got into a fight in the market on his way home yesterday. He was a real hothead in his youth, but has mellowed somewhat with age. The market was crowded and there were two long lines at the registers. The man in his twenties in front of him pointed to his place in line, said, "This is my spot," and then walked outside to smoke a cigarette. When he came back inside he was very loud and cussing in front of women and children. Spence doesn't take well to men cussing in front of women and children, and told him that he needed to calm down. The guy told Spence that it was none of his business and Spence replied, "You <u>better</u> calm down." That's when Spence thought the guy was going to start fighting, but he didn't. When the unruly guy left, the man in line behind Spence said, "I thought there was going to be a fight there. I had your back."

Spence told us about when his wife Sharon and his cousin were sitting at the kitchen table talking about what they would put in a personal ad for an ideal man. His cousin was going on and on about the kind of man she wanted: tall, handsome, dark hair and so on. When she finally finished and it was Sharon's turn to compose her personal ad, Spence interrupted before she could speak one word and said, "Six Cocke County men needed to carry a coffin for a dead woman." Then he told us that his cousin was "laughing like a hen that just laid an egg." After that comment, I was laughing like a hen that had just laid an egg too.

Andy got out the 100-foot measuring tape so we could measure the length of the bridge and the width of Big Creek under it. The bridge is 88 feet 5 inches long and the creek is 59 feet wide between the bridge piers.

- *People coming down a trail were reporting that a seventh-grade girl had been bitten on the hand by a copperhead snake. Eventually, the medic sent to investigate caught up with the girl and said that she was not showing any signs of a severe reaction. She had been bitten on the finger and the hand was swollen – only to her wrist. Dispatch called for an ambulance. Sometime later, the medic reported that she was sending the girl to the hospital.*

- *A maintenance person in Cade's Cove reported that a park visitor told him that a car was driving fast and recklessly and nearly ran over his two daughters who were on bicycles. They had a tag number and said the car was a red classic Chevy of the 1950s vintage. When the Chevy driver saw that they were trying to read his tag, he took off at high speed. A ranger waited at the exit to Cade's Cove to intercept. He kept calling back for a better description of the car and to reaffirm the tag number. I asked Andy, "How many 1950s red Chevys can there be in Cade's Cove at the same time?" The ranger called in again and asked, "Did the car have a white top?" It was a convertible, so the top probably was white. I realized what his problem was when the ranger said there was a classic car club touring the park and there were a lot of 1950s Chevys driving by. He did eventually pull one over and the last we heard about it he was giving dispatch the driver's license number.*

- *A park employee told dispatch that he was "not going to do anything. That turkey looks like he is going to make it through the day."*

We drove back to the Walgreen's in Newport in the late afternoon to pick up Andy's prescription. Then we stopped in the

Subway where Andy bought us each a soda and I did a send/receive of the email. I did not read the email there, but did note one from Sue, our neighbor in Marathon. She said that Mac would be in the mountains today. Darn, it was already late in the day and we missed him. As we were driving along the Pigeon River on our return to Big Creek, a guy on a motorcycle passed us going the other way. Andy said, "That guy on the motorcycle waved to us." I had not mentioned the email to him and replied, "Its Mac." Sure enough, I saw him turning around in the rear view mirror. I pulled over in the parking lot for the raft and kayak launch and Mac pulled in behind us. Andy was stunned. How did I know it was Mac? I don't think I ever confessed.

- *BOLO for a green Kawasaki motorcycle stolen by a person a few days before who was known to carry weapons and drugs. The rangers on duty then gave their call numbers to signify that they had heard the message.*

- *A commercial tractor-trailer was stopped by a ranger for driving in the park. After the driver was given a ticket, the ranger escorted him out of the park. We heard this occasionally, especially if there was an accident on I-40 and truckers were looking for an alternate route.*

The park rules had changed. Campers were only allowed to bring in store-bought kiln-dried firewood with a government seal on it. I was watching to see how that would change camper behavior. They expected to be able to buy firewood in the campground or close by. Neither of those options were available in Big Creek. The closest was the convenience store at the Hartford exit off I-40.

The Daddy Long Legs arrived, or came out, or whatever they do. We counted a dozen of them on the inside of the screen room while we were eating our dinner.

I mentioned to Larry that he appears quite dull in my journals and he should tell me something about himself. He was 67 and a Gatlinburg native, born in the house on the corner at the exit from the Roaring Fork Motor Nature Trail. I supposed Gatlinburg was a much smaller town then.

Then Larry told me about himself and his brother hunting for rabbits in a big field that is now a shopping mall. They had a couple dogs out in the field chasing rabbits while the boys stood on a rise watching the dogs. Larry's brother had his gun down by his side, with his arm relaxed. A rabbit came out of a hole and put his nose right up to the barrel of the gun. They must have been quite surprised; Larry said his brother did not shoot the rabbit. I bet that was a great family story, embellished and repeated over the years.

Larry also told us about going off to college, enlisting in the Marines, and going to Vietnam. He moved to Washington, DC for a year or so and worked for a restoration company. They did some restoration in the Watergate complex after the incident that made it famous.

He told us of a project at the Dulles Airport terminal building. They were using a new machine to spray some product onto the underside of the huge overhang on the front of the terminal. Larry said the product probably worked well in the lab, but it was clogging up the machine on site. They tried to add some silicone to keep it from clogging. Then, the product was dripping onto a big, new, shiny fire engine. The fire marshal was most displeased. The project engineer got some acetone to clean off the windshield of the fire truck. It ran down the front of the truck and red paint flowed onto the pavement. The project went way over budget and the company was sued. Larry thought the president of the company got himself on some review board or committee and the charges were dropped. Larry came back to Tennessee.

- *BOLO for a robbery suspect in a Black 1997 Cadillac Escalade with twenty-inch chrome wheels and a gray interior. The subject, a white male named Michael, had lots of tattoos with a Chinese symbol on the back of his neck. The suspect was ostensibly attempting to sell the Escalade when he choked and robbed the victim of his money and left him at a gas station in Sevierville.*

12

Front Versus Back Country

Edward Abbey is perhaps America's preeminent environmentalist. Always insightful, usually very curmudgeonly, some of his best writing has to do with the national parks. He was a park ranger at Arches National Park in the late 1960s. His essay, "Polemic: Industrial Tourism & The National Parks," first published in his seminal book "Desert Solitaire," is exceptionally acerbic. Funny too, in parts. He chronicles the coming of the paved road in Arches and laments what that means—an end to his peaceful existence as a ranger. Because with roads come people.

One of the things I quickly learned was that there were actually two parts to any national park: the front country versus the back country. The front country is the part Abbey despised. The people, the roads, the campgrounds, the electricity, the flush toilets. It's the part of a national park that most people know and think of as a "national park."

The back country is the still somewhat wild part—the one where the bears and elk still roam somewhat freely, where you can hike a trail and sometimes find that huge silence that fills a mountain when no one but you is there to hear it.

Is the one better than the other? For those who want their wilderness experience intact, they're going to say "of course. The back country is the only way to go." For those who don't want to, or can't, experience the back country, the front country does just fine. I like them both. Andy and I live in an RV after all. We like the experience of driving a road and experiencing the country through our window. But we also like to stop, a lot, and enjoy the moment, the place where we find ourselves.

The first year we hosted in the Great Smokies, we took off on Mondays to shop for groceries and do our laundry in the ranger station. Ranger Tim suggested that we needed to take off another day for some fun. Why didn't we think of that?

We ended up taking full advantage. Although we are excessively dedicated campground hosts, we left home base, Big Creek, to see what other wonders the Great Smoky Mountains National Park offered. It wasn't lost on me that I would have seen "nothing" had paved roads through the park not existed.

Our first big foray was an overnight stay in Cade's Cove, the most popular section of the park. The cove is a wide valley surrounded by mountains and filled with open fields and forest. An eleven-mile single-lane loop road takes you to old log cabins, barns, churches, and a working gristmill, as well as numerous outbuildings. It is a great disappointment in humanity to see how many idiots have carved their names into the logs. The open fields are great for wildlife viewing. We saw a bear in a tree, numerous deer, and turkeys.

The highest point in the park is Clingman's Dome and the lookout tower. This is where I went to get my picture of green mountains in the foreground fading into blue, gray, and then smoky ridges in the distance— the "classic shot" that most everyone who visits the park wants to get. Unfortunately, every time we visited, my view was of clouds or a monsoon rain. We did take the opportunity to hike a bit on the Appalachian Trail from Newfound Gap where I discovered the unforgettable Indian Pipes—plants that are ghostly white because they feed off the fungi in the soil. It was atop the Rockefeller Memorial that I got a view of many Eastern Hemlock trees that have been killed by the Hemlock Woolly Adelgid. The park is battling these insects with funding from the Great Smoky Mountains Association.

The Oconaluftee Visitor Center and Mountain Farm Museum, near the Cherokee, North Carolina entrance to the park, opened in the spring of 2011. The visitor center houses excellent exhibits on early mountain culture, including a still for making moonshine. This is my favorite place in the park because, even though all but the barn were moved from other locations, it looks and feels like a real farm. They even have fields, animals, and a garden. The centerpiece is the Davis House, built from huge Chestnut boards before the Chestnut blight of the nineteen-thirties and forties killed all the trees. Mingus

Mill, built in 1886, is just up the road into the park. At first, I thought the water wheel was missing, but learned that the mill was high-tech and driven by a steel turbine powered by the water from the creek.

Cataloochee is a remote valley that was home to about twelve hundred people in 1910. Part of the adventure is the long, narrow and winding road to get there. There are two ways to get to Cataloochee and neither of them are for the faint of heart. There are several old homes, a barn, churches and a schoolhouse still there. The Caldwell House, built between 1898 and 1903 by Hiram Caldwell is most impressive. It is a large two-story farmhouse with a wrap-around porch and beautiful, elaborate woodwork on the floors, walls, ceilings, and trim. I would move in there with the bats tomorrow. The Cataloochee Valley is where a herd of twenty-five elk was reintroduced in 2001 and another twenty-seven in 2002. Now there are about two hundred and they are expanding their range. Elk are regularly seen in Oconaluftee and occasionally in Big Creek.

Our visit to the Roaring Fork Motor Nature Trail was a bit disappointing because there were no empty parking places at most of the sites (Abbey would have been horrified). The one-lane, one-way road meanders through the mountain forest. It is a beautiful primeval forest, though, and warrants another attempt in the future.

One day we drove around the east/south side of the park to the Blue Ridge Parkway. The Balsam Mountain campground might be the prettiest in the park. It is certainly the highest by far at 5,310 feet. It is remote too, which makes it a good place to get away from it all in the front country. From there, we drove on to Bryson City and visited the Deep Creek area of the park. One must run a gauntlet of inner-tube rental companies to reach the large campground. We visited the campground hosts and then hiked the short-but-steep trail to Juney Whank Falls. Funny name, but they were wonderful with a beautiful log bridge crossing part way up the falls.

I love waterfalls and I always get my fill when I spend time in the Great Smokies. We had noticed the cars overflowing the parking area and along both sides of the road at the Laurel Falls Trailhead every time we passed by. My sister Barbara wanted to see the falls when she visited after having read about the woman in a wheelchair who had fallen off the trail. It was quite a hike, paved-but-rough, a bit over a mile steadily up hill and winding through mountain laurel and rhododendron. Signs warn of bear activity and the steep drop-off right at the edge of the pavement in places. It was enough to take my breath away. The falls are eighty feet high and the trail crosses them about half way up.

We also took Tom and Barbara to Mingo Falls, which are not actually in the park, but on the Cherokee Reservation. The park waterfall book includes them because they are so spectacular and so close, just outside the park. It is a moderately difficult half a mile through rhododendrons to reach the 120-foot falls. Well worth the stairs. The Cherokee Reservation abuts the North Carolina side of the park. The reservation is made up of the Eastern Band of the Cherokee nation who escaped the forced "Trail of Tears" march. Having them by the park is reminder of the long and unsettled history of Native Americans and the part they played in the creation of America—and by extension our parks. They have an excellent museum, well worth a visit.

Our daughter, Kathy, and I walked to Abrams Falls, a five-mile moderate-to-difficult round trip. This waterfall is only about twenty feet high, but the stream is wide and there is a lot of water flowing. The beautiful pool beneath the falls look appealing, but there have been many drownings there due to the fast-moving water. Before we left, Spence reminded us that people get hurt on the trail too. I heard it on the radio regularly. Then I proved it by tripping over a tree root and smacking my face on a rock. No permanent damage.

Spence was back to work after his weekend. When I asked him how it went, he told us that he had played in a fundraiser, memorial golf tournament. Spence loves to play golf, but had not done so in over a year. The memorialized had been one of his foursome that had played every weekend for years. Spence said that he is not a good golfer, but he enjoys drinking the beer that makes him feel better after missing a shot. Andy and Spence talked about golf and the tournament for a while until Spence declared, "Golf is a sissy game anyway. It's not like the manly sports we used to play, like cow pasture football. The best part was when you got to mash the other guy's face in a cow pie." Eeeewww!

We headed up to the tent campground and Spence got his leaf blower to blow the leaves off our outdoor mat.

- ***An elderly woman had fallen off the trail and become wedged between some rocks near Little River Road. They thought she had hit her head. A rescue team was assembled to get her out.***

Spence must have stayed awake in the night thinking up more things to gross me out. He and Andy were sitting outside with their coffee in the morning and, when I came outside to join them, they were talking about football again. Well, as though they had been talking about football anyway - Spence said, "Yeah. The important part of cow pasture football is to find fresh cow pies. The main objective is to smash the other guy's face into a fresh cow pie on the first play. The second objective is to keep your own face from getting mashed into a fresh cow pie." Eeeewww! Spence succeeded in grossing me out twice in two days and was rather proud of himself.

Scout Troop 1882 from Knoxville's Beulah Methodist Church was all packed up in the group site. When they had all left except one man and his son, I walked over to compliment them on how well behaved the boys were. He appreciated the remark and said they had to stay after the boys to not get too wild and hurt themselves out in the forest. He also told me that they made a change in their camping operation this time. They did not bring any paper plates and cups, or any plastic utensils and water bottles. It made an amazing difference in the amount of trash they generated. They usually have two large garbage bags of trash for an overnight campout. This time they only had two small trash bags.

- *One ranger called another and said, "I have the half-burned tickets you issued." He also had something else the people had thrown out the window. Some other park visitors witnessed it and retrieved it. Then he said, "You are going to have some other charges to make."*

Heath pulled into the parking lot and I told him, "I bet you aren't going to be coming to visit us anymore." He immediately quipped, "Why? Did your oven break?" I wanted to know who told him, but he said he was just being funny. Heath never forgets Andy's monthly birthday cake. Unless we got the oven fixed in the next week or so, it would be banana pudding for the May birthday. The meringue might not be browned though.

Spence was a weed-whacking demon. He was working around the parking lot as we walked through. When he saw me with the camera, he idled the weed whacker and yelled, "I told you not to take a picture of me when I'm working!" It would ruin his reputation. Everyone knows he works hard; his reputation is for his attitude.

- *There was a hit-and-run in the evening. They were describing a vehicle with some damage and likely some paint transfer. There were two conversations with dispatch, one with the ranger on the scene and another with a rangers searching for the party who fled. The ranger on scene called for an ambulance for the passenger in the victim car.*

We were surprised to see Spence driving the Gator as we were walking up to the campground two hours past his quitting time. Spence said he had been helping some regular campers pack up to leave. Then he said he really got some sweet talk in the picnic area. There was a story there.

He was weed whacking and mowing that week, getting the park in shape for the Memorial Day holiday weekend. He was working in the picnic area in the afternoon. A man and woman were sitting at the extra-long group picnic table near the parking lot. He told them that, if they moved to a table next to the creek, he would not disturb them. But, they stayed where they were while he used the leaf-blower to clear the debris off the handicap sidewalk behind the group table. He was all the way up to the water fountain near the handicap parking spaces when the woman approached him.

"Thank you very much, you disgusting, despicable, ugly, little man for ruining my picnic!"

Spence was stunned. He could not believe she said that and had already walked on before coming up with his retort: "You are not a very nice person either." He had warned them that he was going to be working there and had suggested a simple solution.

I started laughing and had him repeat the sentence until I got it right on my voice recorder. When he saw that he got me laughing, he continued his rant.

"I know I ain't a purty boy, but hell far!"

I was hysterical. Andy and Spence spent the next twenty minutes coming up with ripostes he might have used and I added a few quips of my own. Of course, park employees do not get into arguments with park visitors. With that, Spence left for home and we walked around the campground.

Headlights came down to the group site about nine o'clock. Andy went out to see what was going on. It was a group arriving. Shannon and her boyfriend Will were leading a group of college kids on a mountain adventure trip. They were rafting on the Pigeon River the next morning. Shannon and Will were graduate students at the University of Tennessee in Knoxville and were also interpretive rangers in the park.

- ***BOLO for a suicide alert, an armed, 38-year-old man in a 1996 white Chevy pickup truck. Accused of sexually abusing a minor. Has a 22 long-barrel pistol. Last seen in Newport, TN. This announcement was made for officer safety.***

- ***A ranger was continuing on the case where someone tore up the violation notice and threw it out the window at him. Are you kidding me? What kind of idiot would do that?***

Heath told us a story about wild boars. He was driving on the Roaring Fork Motor Nature Trail when he saw a spot on the side of the road that looked as though it had been very recently uprooted by pigs. A moment or two later, Heath saw a sow and a bunch of piglets. He pushed the button to unlock his shotgun and pulled it from behind his seat. Then he got out of his vehicle as quietly as possible. He took aim but had not released the safety. When he did that, the click alerted the sow and she took off running into the woods with the piglets trailing after her. Heath took off after them, firing away, but did not hit anything. And, here is what the story was really about. When he got back to his vehicle, he discovered that he had left it running and in gear. He didn't know why it did not roll down the hill and into the woods. I suppose the slope at that spot was in his favor and saved him from certain humiliation.

The couple in Site 1 had a small, shaggy, wiry-haired dog. She was old, "can't see, and can't hear." The man acknowledged, "She will bite 'cha, but the good news is that she only has two teeth left."

- ***There was an emergency at Parks that might have been a heart problem. The medic on the scene said he was not sure it was a cardiac problem, but the man was unable to walk. The medic started an IV. Later, he reported that the man seemed to be stabilized, but had tightness in his chest.***

- *BOLO for four missing persons in a 1998 white Chevy van. The woman picked up her three children from school on the 13th of May and advised someone that she was driving to an unknown destination in Gatlinburg. The children were aged nine, seven, and three. Later, a ranger reported the van was in the Elkmont campground. Later in the evening, however, dispatch announced that she was faxing more information to all rangers about the children in the BOLO.*

- *A ranger in Cade's Cove noted that a window was missing in the Methodist Church.*

The motorhome black water (sewage) holding tank would not drain. I was complaining about the holding tank problem we were experiencing while we drank our coffee in the morning and ended my lament with, "I like my toilet. You never know what might be lurking in the toilet building." Spence agreed, "I like my toilet." Then he told us about working on the trail crew years ago and felt the urge to go. Of course, he went into the forest. He was still zipping and buttoning as he walked back to the trail. As he cinched his belt, he felt stings. The rest of the trail crew had a good laugh while Spence ripped off his pants and underwear and danced on the trail. He had squatted over a yellow-jacket nest.

We saw aluminum cans in the nearly-empty dumpster as we took out the trash in the morning. They were too far down to reach so I suggested to Andy that we hold Spence by his ankles so he could retrieve them. Spence saves any aluminum cans he picks up around the park and sells them to the recycle man. I had begun picking them up and collecting them from campers for him in addition to the ones we empty ourselves. Some campers ask why the park does not recycle so I asked Spence. He told us the park tried recycling in the past, but park visitors put trash in the recycle bins.

We heard another Sharon story. One of Spence's buddies was playing in a band and invited Spence to come along on a gig at a bar somewhere in Cocke County. Spence was dating Sharon at the time and took her along. The music was loud. When Sharon said something to Spence, he could not hear her. Several times, she spoke, he said, "what?" and leaned closer. When he was leaning in really close he could clearly hear her say, "You are spilling your beer in my crotch."

A lively group of six men returned to Site 12. We remembered them and they remembered us from the previous year. They had been meeting in Big Creek for the past thirty years during the week before the Memorial Day holiday weekend. We enjoyed them before and I was looking forward to chatting with them when we walked around the campground. They were ready for rain with huge blue tarps hung over the tent, picnic table, and fire ring. One of them was a chef, so they would be eating well.

The men in Site 12 told us the one toilet in the men's room was stopped up. I called dispatch on the radio to report it. He told me to stand by while he contacted someone from maintenance. I chatted with the Site 12 guys until dispatch called me back to say our maintenance man would come in. That meant Spence.

We saw Spence's pickup truck coming down the road so I went to the door as he and Richard got out of the truck. I didn't think it was a job for two men. Spence asked, "Has your water come back on?" What? It's not a water problem, it's a stopped up toilet. That explained why Richard came along; he was the water system expert. I offered coffee and they said they would take care of the men's room and be back.

When the coffee was poured, Andy and I started telling Richard about the woman who called Spence a disgusting, despicable, ugly, little man for ruining her picnic. Then I told him I laughed even harder when Spence said, "I know I ain't a purty boy, but hell far!" Then I admitted that it was mean of me to laugh when Spence had been abused for working. Richard reckoned that she broke his heart so I showed him the picture I took of Spence when he was telling us what happened.

Spence looked at his picture and said, "It looks like a red worm with the poop slung out of it." (He didn't actually say "poop").

"It looks like <u>what</u>?"

He added, "That's what people say when you look like that." I suppose that means sad or having hurt feelings.

Richard agreed, "Yeah, that's what people say." Oh my gosh, I had never heard an expression like that one. My eastern North Carolina family used many colorful expressions too, but I never hear them anymore. Our speech is much duller now.

There was another first for me in the campground Wednesday morning. An exceptionally pleasant Buddhist monk was camped in Site 5. His buddy was studying the trail map so Andy gave them hiking advice.

- *Dispatch announced that a turkey had been hit by a car and was flopping around in the road and "disturbing people." Well, the people were probably not half as disturbed as the poor turkey. Some rangers were going to get it off the road.*

- *A large black male bear was hanging around the Laurel Falls trail. The Laurel Falls Rover could not convince it to leave and called for help. Several voices chimed in saying they were on the way. Later, a ranger called in to say the bear was gone and it was not the same bear that had been there in the morning.*

- *Three or four rangers were responding to an incident on the Foothills Parkway. Blount County had reported it to the park. A man and woman were at an overlook having a fight. Witnesses reported seeing the man strike the woman. Later, someone said the man had left the park. One park ranger was going to check out the scene to see if the woman or witnesses were still there.*

A young woman came to the door asking what to do. They had set up on Site 3, but did not have the cash. Her father was on the way with a credit card so she could get some cash at an ATM. Andy told her to put the tab on the board and keep the envelope until she had the cash, and then put the envelope in the iron ranger. When we walked up to the registration board, two notes were put up instead of envelope tabs. The young woman from Site 3 put up this note written on a comment card.

"There's three of us. The camp host told us to go ahead & set up. We have to go get money out of the ATM. I talked to the old nice man up front in the RV."

"Old nice man! She can't be talking about me; I'm only 78!"

The other note was from the folks who had moved into Site 10.

"Dropped camping permit and money in the box!
Campsite 10 Cody
5-21-15 to 5-22-15
4 people/1 night"

They could not just take another pay envelope out of the slot, because the slot was empty. I put more than enough envelopes for every campsite to turn over every day. They must be using them to start campfires. The same was true for the Smokies Guide newspapers. If I set a stack of them at the registration board, they would disappear in a heartbeat. So I began carrying them in my camp-host satchel and handing them out to new campers. I had brought some envelopes with me and gave the woman one to fill out and put on the board.

The two men in Site 5 were cooking breakfast in a huge stockpot full of noodles and vegetables, easily enough for a family of ten. If that monk ate like that all the time, he'd be a Buddha real soon.

When we got to Site 12, Andy was complaining about the note and being called an old nice man. One of the guys quipped, "What? She said you are nice?"

A woman told us she saw a bear next to the toilet building when she took a late-night trip. One of the men in Site 11 said he saw one in the woods uphill from the campground. Both of them described it as a small bear, so it must have been the same bear. We reminded everyone to keep a clean campsite so as not to invite the bear into the campground.

- *BOLO for a white male, 25 years of age. He had a weapon and had said that he would shoot any law enforcement people he came in contact with. He was traveling with a male companion. He was also a known meth producer, seller, and user.*
- *BOLO for a green Chevy Cavalier. The police were called for a domestic dispute, but the couple had left home with a small child before the police could get there. The rangers were instructed to make a welfare check if they spotted the car.*

Heath stopped in after he had transported some hikers from Cosby back to Big Creek. I served him some of Andy's birthday banana pudding. Then I asked him, when he was a child, did he want to be a park ranger when he grew up. How did he become one?

Young Heath and his wife Dana were happy with their seasonal jobs in the park. They had worked a number of different kinds of jobs. Then, when Dana got pregnant, he realized he needed a year-round job. The man who had been his football coach told him to apply for a position as a police officer in Gatlinburg. After a few years, he got tired of arresting the same drunk and wanted to go back to work for the park. He just happened to be talking to the man who was the head of the park's dispatch office at the time. He told Heath that they were going to be hiring and Heath should get qualified as a dispatcher, which would give him an advantage. The baby is going to college now and Heath still loves his job as a park ranger.

I was making chili for our dinner and had invited Spence to join us. He and Andy were sitting outside while I was cooking. I heard Spence call to a backpacker walking down the horse trail. We had seen a car parked in the horse camp day lot for nearly a week and were hoping someone returned to it soon. I asked if that was his blue car and he said yes. The guys started talking about his hike and Andy invited him to eat chili with us. He quickly accepted and set down his backpack.

While we were eating, we heard Heath on the radio saying he was in Big Creek. Andy, Spence, and I all laughed and said Heath smelled the chili. A moment later, dispatch told Heath some hikers had found camping gear along the Baxter Creek Trail. They had brought it to the ranger station. My thought was that a hiker had set his gear down to find a private spot behind some trees to take care of business. He was probably not happy to return to the trail to find his gear gone. Heath told us later, that the gear was actually spread along the trail. He put it in the ranger station so we could return it to the owner if they came to claim it. No one ever did. It was another Big Creek mystery.

Then Heath got another call. Park visitors had called the park to report that someone had left a dog in the back of their pickup truck (with a cap) while they hiked up the Big Creek Trail. Andy and Spence headed up to the parking lot to see if they could rescue the dog. Hiker Jeff loaded up his backpack, thanked me for the chili, which he said was better than his mother's, and headed on down the trail to his car. Andy returned to the RV for a tarp to put over the back of the pickup to shade it a bit. The truck cap had a small open window, but the dog was still hot. Its tongue was hanging out, but it was not panting. I wrote a courtesy notice and put it on their windshield.

I walked around the campground while Andy, Heath, and Spence stayed in the parking lot. Cars arrived every few minutes with people looking for a campsite or just a place to park. I also spent some time directing traffic when I got back to the parking lot. That means telling some people the campground was full and telling others where they could find a parking space. Heath had left without eating any chili.

- *A couple had called the park for help when their twelve-year-old son did not return to the Smokemont campsite after heading out into the forest near the Toe String trail looking for firewood. A team was formed to search for him. Some personnel were assigned to keep park visitors out of the area so they would not destroy any signs of the boy's track. Ranger Will told us the boy was found. It was several hours after he went missing before I lost track of it on the radio.*

- *A two-year-old fell at Clingman's Dome and her head was bleeding. She was not responding, but they did not think she was unconscious. Her eyes were open. Dispatch decided to send EMS. A few minutes later, they reported that it was just a scrape on the chin and she seemed better. Later, the little girl was not as responsive as before. Will told us she was fine.*

- *About noon, an off-duty ranger reported that there was a cardiac event on the Laurel Falls trail. They were giving him CPR. He had a history of heart disease and high blood pressure. He was not conscious. Will told us the man had died. I wondered whether there was a way to prevent people with bad hearts or otherwise not in good shape to attempt some of the trails. Maybe some warning signs with a description of the trail at the trailhead. I had heard of too many heart attacks on the radio.*

- *Just before 6:00, the elk were wandering around near the Mingus Mill and traffic was building up. Dispatch called for the Luftee Rover to control traffic.*

- *That evening a ranger said he was going to be out with an individual who was wearing camouflage and lying in a pullout. That got our attention. A moment or two later he came back on the radio to say it was not camouflage, but actually very dirty clothes. He talked to the young man and learned that he was walking over the mountain to Cherokee. The ranger told him it is dangerous to walk on the narrow mountain road in the dark so the man showed him a blinking flashlight. The rangers can warn someone, but they can't stop him from doing something dangerous.*

- *A ranger came upon some people camping illegally (not in a campground) and told them to move on. I don't know where else they could go in the park; it seemed all the campgrounds were full.*

Dispatch stayed hopping-busy late into the evening responding to ranger's traffic stops for all kinds of reasons. He was still answering one call after the other when I finished my journal shortly before midnight.

The next morning, Spence stopped by for a cup of coffee and brought me a bucket of sour cherries from the trees in his yard. I began to pit them in the morning, but we were so busy with park visitors that I didn't finish until afternoon.

Andy and Spence both spent a large part of the day in the parking lot directing visitors to park in the horse camp day-use lot. Some still parked illegally. One couple had a small dog with them and Andy told them we would dog-sit while the family hiked. They arrived at our site and I fell in love. She was a designer dog, half poodle and half something else. She was still a puppy, all wiggle and lick, and her name was Abbey. She yipped for a while after her family left, but then calmed down. She was busy watching down the horse trail and up to the road whenever there were people or vehicle sounds, looking for them to return. Andy took a chair out to the mossy lawn to keep her company and she jumped into his lap.

It was late in the afternoon before I got the cherries prepared. There was not enough for a pie, so I planned on a tart. Part way through prep, I simply dumped the cherries into a pie plate and spooned my slightly wet dough on top. I did not use a recipe for the cherries or the crust so I was a bit apprehensive about how it would turn out. I pulled it out of the oven and walked up to the parking lot to tell Andy and Spence it was done. Heath was in the parking lot. How did he know? Ranger Chase was with him and was writing some parking tickets. In both cases, the people parked right in front of the No Parking signs. When they were finished with the tickets, all four men came to our site for my cherry concoction. It was delicious.

- *Just before noon, there was a two-mile traffic backup on the Roaring Fork Motor Nature Trail. Someone had parked a car partially in the road and cars could not get by. Another voice said to close the gate so that no more cars could enter and then see if some of the ones stuck could turn around and come back out. The reporting party said that a large man was attempting to pick up the car enough to move it off the road. The Roaring Fork Motor Nature Trail is an extremely narrow, one-way, paved road through a mountainside forest. There are old cabins, waterfalls, and plants. There are a few spots for parking and maybe some pull-offs, but very little opportunity to pass the car in front of you. I have no idea how long it took to clear up that jam. I'm calling that one a jerk jam.*

- *A ranger called in a vehicle license for some people who had a passenger riding on the bumper of a Chevy Blazer. I pictured the person standing on the back bumper and holding on to the luggage rack on top of the vehicle. Yee ha!*

- *A bear in the Chimneys picnic area took food from a picnic table. The reporting party said he ran him off into the woods, but he would come back. The wildlife person responding said he was on his way with a trap. Another bear was just past the Methodist Church in Cades Cove. Yet another bear was in the stables at Cades Cove. It left on its own before the wildlife people could get there to chase it away.*

- *There was a two-motorcycle accident near Look Rock. The ranger called it in as an emergency and asked for EMS. He said there were three people who would need an ambulance. Later, he called again and asked for Life Star, the helicopter ambulance.*

- *Wildlife specialists, 355 and 344, were planning to meet somewhere and net bats. That called for a bit of research so I checked the park website.*

White Nose Syndrome is killing millions of bats across the US. It is caused by a fungus, Pseudogymnoascus destructans, which was found in a cave in the Great Smoky Mountains

National Park in 2010. When a bat is infected with this fungus, it gets a frothy white coating on its nose, ears, and wings. The current theory is that the fungus irritates the bats and causes them to be restless and burn more body fat than normal and then not have enough to survive the winter. If a bat wakes too early, it can freeze to death or starve. Another thought is that the fungus causes dehydration, which damages membranes on bat's wings. Bats in the northeast have had ninety percent mortality due to white nose syndrome. There are at least eleven species of bats in the park, including the federally endangered Indiana Bat and the Rafinesque's Big-Eared Bat, of concern to both North Carolina and Tennessee. The most common is the Little Brown Bat. If white nose syndrome continues to spread at its current rate, the Little Brown Bats could be regionally extinct within twenty years. All sixteen caves and several mines in the Great Smoky Mountains National Park have been closed to park visitors in an attempt to protect the bats.

This is not just a crisis for the bats, but for us as well. A single Little Brown Bat eats a thousand mosquitoes and other insects in an hour. A nursing female can eat her weight in insects each night. Bats also eat many night-flying crop pests. This is critical for agriculture and our forests. In addition to eating insects, bats pollinate plants, spread seeds, and serve as prey for weasels, minks, raccoons, owls, hawks, snakes, and even spiders.

- *In the evening, a ranger reported that he was following a motorcycle going at a high rate of speed. We could hear his siren wailing. He said the biker would not stop and that he was passing multiple cars. The bike was headed north on US 441 from Cherokee. Other rangers chimed in and would place themselves in position to pursue the motorcycle. One blocked the road with his car, but the biker swerved and went around it. Then the biker made a U-turn and headed back toward Cherokee. Dispatch called Cherokee police to be at that end of the park, and then set the radios so the Cherokee police could hear the park rangers. Other rangers were closing gates to prevent the motorcycle from driving on side roads. Four Cherokee units reached Smokemont, but had not seen the motorcycle. Then they were sure that the biker had ducked off the road somewhere. One reported that there was a big black mark on the road at the Smokemont campground. The biker ditched the bike and ran into woods. We could hear the ranger huffing and puffing as he was reporting and then we heard him say, "one apprehended." It was a Honda motorcycle with Wisconsin plates. The guy had a Florida driver's license. Like most other events on the radio, there came a point when the rangers were not talking to dispatch anymore. We never heard any more about it except when 518 called in the license numbers. We'll never know why he didn't stop for the ranger in the first place.*

I always supposed that Sunday was the busiest day in Big Creek with family and church groups arriving for picnics. But Memorial Day beat any Sunday we had seen. Cars already filled the picnic area lot as we walked to the campground for our morning walkaround.

The nurse in Site 8 met us to tell us what happened in the campground in the night. The groups in Sites 10 and 11 were both drinking and partying late into the night. There was also a visitor in Site 10. About 2:00 a.m., an argument broke out and a young woman stormed off and spun gravel all the way out of the parking lot and was part way down the campground road when she hit one of the boulders lining the side of the road. The nurse checked on her. She had hit her head and her pickup was atop a boulder with both rear wheels off the ground. The nurse told us that the woman was very drunk so she took her keys to prevent her from driving any more. Of course, from the picture she showed us of the truck atop a boulder with at least three wheels off the ground, I'm sure she was not going anywhere anyway. Apparently; the garbage truck had pulled her off the rock in the morning. The young men in Site 11 were gone and the group in Site 10 was packing up. Other than a huge knot on the girl's forehead, the big casualty in the incident was the new no-parking sign. The post was broken and, the sign was lying in the woods.

A steady flood of cars was pouring into Big Creek. Andy and Spence stationed themselves near the entrance to our site and told people to go to the horse camp. Andy and Spence continued directing traffic while I walked down to the horse camp to assess the situation there. I noticed a horse trailer in the midst of the cars.

They had all parked their cars so close to it that the horse owners would not be able to open the doors to load their horses. Even if they could load them, they could not drive out. There were three spaces left, which filled up as I counted them. Boss Larry came by and said I could tell people to park in the band of grass on the perimeter of the lot. Spence was not too happy to hear that; he takes care of that grass.

A couple drove in with a large dog. Andy told them they could not take it on the trail and offered my services as a dog sitter. His name was Butch and he was a brute; a mix of Boxer and English bulldog. He was also a very well behaved sweetie. I took my book, a mug of iced tea, and a park radio with me and sat with Butch under a tree. He fell in love with me right away, after I fed him bits of a cheese stick.

Spence arrived for a cold drink and a break. He said he had cleaned all the toilet buildings twice. We saw two horses come down the trail and Spence jumped up to tell the man that he might be blocked in at the parking lot.

They rode on to the parking area and were, indeed, still blocked in. They rode back to our site and the man was furious. "What kind of idiot would block a horse trailer like that?" or, words to that effect. Andy got on the Gator with Spence and they all went back to the horse camp to wait for the idiot. Andy told me later that Spence had the couple laughing with his antics in short order. They were calm when the very nice people arrived and apologized to Spence who said, "Don't apologize to me; apologize to them." They just were not thinking in their desperate search for a parking space. They moved their car and the horseman was able to back his trailer out to load the horses.

- *A car was on the side of the road and had run out of gas. Butler's Towing was called to deliver some. Later the ranger called in again to say that the woman took off without paying for the gas. She did not have the cash to pay the man so she was supposedly following the tow truck to Townsend, Tennessee to pay with a credit card. She dropped back and the truck driver lost sight of her in his rear view mirror on the curves. He pulled over in a pull-off to wait for her to catch up. Then he turned around to look for her and she was nowhere to be found. There are only so many places to hide in the park and, about half an hour later, another ranger called in to say he was following the car in the back loop of a campground; then he pulled her over. They arrested the woman and called the tow truck company to come impound the car.*

Finally, in the evening the madness calmed down. Spence went home and we went to the motorhome. It was just about dark when I invited Andy on a walk to the dumpster in the parking lot. It was such a beautiful evening; I suggested that we walk out on the bridge. We saw a light across the creek. My first thought was that we had illegal campers over there, but the bobbing light came across the bridge toward us.

The two young women had been on a backcountry hike for a few days and had arrived at Campsite 38 on Mount Sterling. They were eating when a medium sized bear rushed in and snatched Rachel's pack. It carried the pack into the woods and then came back for more. Apparently the bear was not afraid of people and reared up on its hind legs and roared at them. Rachel assured us that she probably screamed much louder than the bear. The bear did leave, likely with a headache. Rachel and Jessica, as well as all the other campers there, were terrified. Everyone decided to leave. Rachel and Jessica ran down the steep, six-mile Baxter Creek Trail until it was too dark to go fast. I mean that literally; they are trail runners. They were excited and exhausted when they crossed the bridge and ran into us.

I called dispatch to report the incident and we brought the women back to the motorhome. It was a bit too much excitement for all of us. I offered them something to drink while they told their story.

We told them that we had heard rangers or wildlife people on the radio who escorted campers back to the scene of bear incidents. Rachel was anxious to get the top part of her pack, which had her cell phone, camera and wallet in it. She had managed to pick up some clothing and her sleeping bag and stuffed them into a mesh sack, which she reported to be very difficult to carry slung over her shoulder while running down a mountain.

They wanted to stay to get her valuables, but were not anxious to sleep outside in bear country any more. We offered them our hide-a-bed and they eagerly accepted. They were especially happy to take hot showers. They hopped on the hide-a-bed and Rachel sighed, "Bear proof."

Another couple arrived looking for a place to camp. They were hiking up to Site 38 and had met Rachel and Jessica coming down the trail. They listened to the bear story and decided to continue up the mountain anyway. Then they met other hikers fleeing Site 38 and decided that, perhaps they should not go there after all. They turned around and came to us because the campground was full. We told them to pitch a tent on our mossy lawn. I tried to make them feel welcome and said they could use some of our wood and build a fire in the fire ring.

The next morning, a wildlife person called us on the radio and said that he wanted to interview Rachel on the phone. He gave me a phone number for her to call. She and Jessica loaded their gear and headed to their car to drive down to the river to get a cell phone signal. They returned a short while later to say that the wildlife guy would come help them get the camera, phone, and wallet later in the day. He would call me on the radio when he was coming. Rachel and Jessica decided to go to Gatlinburg and gave me Jessica's phone number to call them when I heard from wildlife.

We headed out on our weekly run for groceries and errands. When we got back home, Rachel and Jessica were parked in the picnic area parking lot. We had heard Spence calling on the radio to see when someone was coming and he was told it would be late afternoon or early evening.

- *Chuck reported that he was at the Mount Sterling trailhead and was heading up to Site 38 to close it. I walked up to the parking lot to report that news to the women. When they figured he had had enough time to reach Site 38, they came to the RV. Soon, we heard Chuck say that he was at Site 38 and was telling everyone to leave. He would transport some back to their cars in Big Creek. I then called Chuck to ask if he found Rachel's things. He said she should go home; he had her contact information and would call her if he found anything. The two very disappointed women left for home. I didn't think Chuck spent too much time looking for the camera, phone, and wallet. He and the campers had hiked back down the Mount Sterling trail and were back at Big Creek before we finished our campground rounds. He was gone when we left the campground and we did not get a chance to ask him about it.*

- *A rockslide was blocking both lanes on Clingman's Dome Road. They were calling for heavy equipment to come clean up the mess. They closed the road. We heard them talking on the radio most of the day and they opened the road to traffic in the evening.*

- *A park visitor reported that a large white cow, as in "moo," was on the Rich Mountain Road, a mile into the park. The ranger and dispatch hardly believed it, but when the ranger got there he called dispatch and reported, "True. White cow." He tried to herd her back out of the park but we didn't hear how successful he was.*

Tuesday was a blessed quiet day in Big Creek to give us time to recover from the holiday weekend. Spence dropped in for a coffee refill. We watched the Camp Carolina group in the group site loading up and heading out with their rafts on top of the school bus. Then Spence got to work and we walked up to the campground.

- *An older man was driving too slowly and the reporting party "only honked the horn once." They were outside their cars and the older man attempted to hit the younger with his cane. The honker apparently stepped aside and the old man hit his own car. We did not hear the old man's side of the story or how the situation was handled by the ranger.*

- *A ranger got a report of a visitor killing and disturbing wildlife. The witness who called in got a car tag number. Later a ranger called in to say the man had killed a rattlesnake and one of the rattles was missing. I didn't hear any more about it and don't know if they caught up with the offender.*

Campers in the group site told me that a toilet in the ladies room in the picnic area was stopped up and running over. I called it in to dispatch, since it was after hours for the Cosby maintenance crew. In the morning, one of the women told me that a toilet in the tent campground ladies room was also stopped up. I called Richard on the radio and he said he would be over to take care of both.

- *A large bull elk was next to the road causing major traffic problems just inside the park near Oconaluftee. Luftee Rovers were sent to deal with him, or at least encourage the park visitors to keep moving. I figure the bull elk was going to do whatever he pleased.*

- *A twenty-year-old woman fell about twenty feet off the trail at Ramsey Cascades, three miles from the trailhead. She had a big gash on her forehead. It took a long time to round up people to help carry the woman out. After a while, they didn't care if people were litter certified, as long as they were strong. Heath was out with the patient at a bridge. He said she was not moving, he must have meant she was not moving down the trail rather than that she was dead. Then they decided to walk her out, but were keeping the litter team on standby, just in case she couldn't make it. Later, the litter crew was moving her down the trail. Later still, they were "off trail," "clear," and the patient was on her way to the hospital.*

- *In the early evening, there was a serious accident on Parsons Branch Road at the far end of the park. The vehicle was a rented Jeep that was on its side in the middle of the road. When the park ranger arrived, there were already emergency vehicles on scene from outside the park. Four passengers were going to the University of Tennessee in Knoxville, one by helicopter and three by ambulance. According to the ranger, there were "beer cans everywhere." One of the ambulance drivers requested another helicopter at 8:24.*

- *The wildlife guys were out late at night checking traps.*

We had closed all the shades and Andy was taking his boots off when we got a knock at the door. An excited young man said that a horse and buggy had fallen off Big Creek Road down past the horse camp and they wanted me to call a ranger. He also said the physician in the group site was going to help.

I called dispatch on the radio to report and said we would go check it out and call back with an update. We drove the car and Andy had the presence of mind to take his flashlight. I left mine in the motorhome. Just at the horse camp entrance, we came upon a group of horses and riders making their way up the road. They said they were not with the others, but had come upon them a while back. Then, we encountered two men walking. They were not hurt and did not want a ranger. One of the men said he wanted a ride down to the stop sign at the park entrance. Our back seat was full of "stuff" so there was only room for two in the car. Andy got out and said he would walk while I drove the man home.

We had not gone far when I saw a light off the down-mountain side of the road and stopped the car. A man, a horse, and a grown boy climbed up over the edge of the road into my headlights. I asked if they were OK, and they were not hurt. The horse kept sticking its head in the car window.

I called dispatch again to report that no one was hurt or wanted help and I was driving the man home. We met the doctor and his son by the ranger station as they were driving back up the road and he asked the man if he wanted the doctor to check him over. He said, "I don't need no doctor." I relayed the message, "He don't need no doctor." Then he told me that some hikers had spooked the horse and that caused the accident.

The others walked down the road. The man wanted Andy's flashlight, but Andy was not willing to part with it. That made the man angry. He told Andy to go away, he wasn't needed. Apparently, he fussed at Andy all the way down the road. After I dropped off my passenger at his house and made my way back up the road, I met the boy with the horse. He apologized, "My dad is drunk and he's been cussin' at your husband." Next, I encountered Andy, who got in the car, livid and ready for a fight.

When we got back to our site, we chatted with the doctor in the group site. I told him the men were drunk and he agreed, "Moonshine, made it himself."

13

Robert Spence

His personality is larger than life. More like a character on a television sit-com. Actually, he has an attitude, as they say, and maybe his character would be more likely found in an edgy comedy movie.

Spence is a scrawny guy; I am always after him to eat more and put on some weight. His park uniform hangs loosely on his frame. His blonde, turning gray, hair is down past his shoulders. He keeps it pulled back in a pigtail under his uniform ball cap so most people probably don't notice it.

After serving him coffee in the mornings and a soda at lunchtime for several years, I began to see where that attitude comes from. Spence has a very strong sense of right and wrong, of good manners, and responsibility. He has little patience for those who do not adhere to his code of conduct. Then, there is that quick temper. Surely, it is not his fault; it's that Scots-Irish blood handed down by his ancestors. They also handed down a strong work ethic. Some might consider the maintenance man at the very bottom of the corporate ladder and they would be surprised how much pride Spence takes in the park. It is evident all around Big Creek.

How can it be that Spence charmed a group of women telling them gross toilet stories? He is a natural born storyteller. A small incident with campers or day visitors can turn into a story. A story told with enthusiasm and animation, with commentary on top. His wry sense of humor can turn the dullest report into an event. The east Tennessee accent and colloquialisms add even more color.

It was common for campers to ask us about Spence as we made our campground rounds. And, I don't mean just the regular, local campers. Those who come once a year or less always ask. They all love him. They take notice of the clean restrooms, trim lawn, ash-less fire rings, and clean sidewalks. Sometimes, when we approached a campsite to introduce ourselves, hand out the Smokies Guide, and give the bear lecture, campers will say that Spence answered their questions. For many, he is the only park employee they will see during their visit to Big Creek.

- **There was a search and rescue going on somewhere in the park. I did not hear what happened, but it took them hours to get a rescue party gathered at the trailhead and hike up with the litter. Maybe just as long to reach the patient. Rescue Ranger Heath was part of the team, as usual. He reported reaching the patient and, within a few minutes, reported that they were heading back down the trail with her on the litter. Much later, I heard him say that they did not need an ambulance; she was leaving in her own car. I guessed it was a broken bone and her companion was going to drive her to a clinic to get her patched up.**

Andy and I walked down Big Creek Road to see if the buggy that followed the horse off the side was still there. It was not. We surmised that the owners had come up with the flat-bed truck I had seen in front of the man's house and pulled the buggy up the mountainside during the night. The location was obvious from the disturbed vegetation. We stood on the side of the road looking down a steep slope. It looked as though a big tree root ball ten or fifteen feet down stopped them from going farther downhill.

Rangers Will and Chase surprised us sitting outside of our motorhome when we got back to the host site. They had walked ten miles over the mountain from Cosby and were waiting for Heath to come pick them up. They have both worked at several different parks and we enjoyed hearing their stories.

We walked along the creek path and spotted a few more saplings that had been cut down for firewood by campers. I may have to move up my forecast for when the campers are going to denude the valley for firewood.

Monday was errand day and we drove to the grocery store in Newport. When we returned to the drive to our campsite, a car with "Just Married" on the back window was parked in front of the gate, the one with the "Do Not Block Gate" sign on it. I put on the turn signal to give them the hint that we wanted to turn in. The people were standing next to the car, but didn't move, so Andy got out of the car and told them, "You can't park here; you are blocking the road." The young bride responded, "It's my car and I'm the customer and I can park it wherever I want." Andy returned, "Well, I can call a ranger and he can discuss that with you." I could hear her from inside the car, "Call the f---ing ranger and I'll call the police!" I guess she didn't realize that rangers are the police. Andy turned to me, "Dinata, call the ranger." At that, the groom told his bride to get back in the car and drove away.

- *A four-foot wall of water had just passed through the Chimneys picnic area. Others, elsewhere in the park, were reporting water levels and warning people wading in the river.*

It was 56 degrees the next morning. Spence stopped by for a coffee refill and told us that the only campers in the campground were the regular "purple-raft people" so we reported eleven vacancies for the morning campground report. After a brief period of sunshine in the morning, it rained or misted most of the cold, dreary day. Loud thunder echoed through the valley. We stayed indoors.

- *A heavy woman had fallen and broken her arm at Abrams Falls. She did not think she would be able to make it out by herself. At 3:50 they were assembling a litter team at the trailhead. Rescue 2 was at the trailhead at 5:22 and reported that they were on the trail at 5:29. They got to the patient at 6:18 and were heading back down the trail in just a few minutes. They requested an ambulance at 7:05, when they thought they were about half an hour from the trailhead. There must have been more than a broken arm; I don't see how that would prevent her from walking out. From this timeline, you can see that help is not going to be there within minutes to whisk you to the emergency room when you get hurt on the trail.*

The next morning, I saw Andy talking with a couple with a dog in the campground parking lot. I did not recognize them right away, but when they introduced themselves, I remembered their name. They were the campground hosts who told us the bear had stolen their sewer hose in 2010. I immediately apologized to Richard for thinking he was a little crazy. I told him about the man with the spray bottle who came out of the woods with a destroyed sewer hose with bear tooth marks on the fittings.

When we talk to campers about not leaving food, or anything with a scent, out to attract bears, we tell them that a woman had told us a bear tore open and drank from a bottle of bleach and a bottle of charcoal lighter fluid. Pat reminded us that she was the one who told us a bear will drink bleach, or at least taste it. Anything with a scent folks.

Richard and Pat had a group in the group site with a bunch of kids screaming and making a lot of noise in the night. Pat said she didn't think anything of it. Just kids playing. The next morning, the adult campers asked if they had heard them and said it was a bear that had torn into all the tents during the night that set off the screaming. A wildlife guy came and set a trap to capture the bear. They figured it was the same bear that stole the sewer hose and tore into the tents.

- *In the evening there was a lot of conversation between numerous rangers searching for a suicidal couple. The man was apparently in trouble and had skipped his bail. Family members had called the park to report them. Dispatch got a phone number and called the man, who said he was in the park near a waterfall, but would not say which one. When he realized that he was talking to a park official, he hung up. The couple was from Gatlinburg and did not have a car, so rangers were checking waterfalls within walking distance from town.*

Local and regular camper, Windy, informed us that we need to be politically correct. He was no longer a hillbilly, but was an Appalachian American.

The people in the group camp left out a lot of coolers and bins so we went over to make sure they had not left out any food. There was a huge frying pan on the camp stove that had been used to scramble eggs. They had filled it to the brim with water. A large assortment of spices and cleaning products was on the table. We took the "kids cooler" full of juices and other liquids in plastic containers and kept it inside the motorhome for safekeeping.

Heath brought his son Garrett over to swim in the Midnight Hole. This was the first time we had seen Heath without a ranger uniform. He was wearing a Boy Scout t-shirt so he was still a good guy.

When the group people returned, Andy went over to give them the bear lecture. One man came and got the frying pan, but did not take the cooler or other foodstuff. Andy went back over to talk to them, but one man said, "Not now; I'm eating my lunch." He did not agree with Andy that they should put the coolers away when they were not being watched. As soon as Heath returned from the Midnight Hole, Andy took him to the group site to talk to the people about bears. Later the group campers hung a tarp between us and their picnic table and grill so we could not see the five or six coolers left out behind it. I half hoped that a bear would come tear them up.

I had heard it on the radio and asked Heath about the missing woman he found dead in a creek. Jenny Bennett had been missing a week. He thought she had been swept away in high water due to the heavy rains. Heath said he stayed with her body for four hours until a litter team got there to take her out. She was a blogger and an author who had written about the park. She was known for hiking off trails and crossing creeks by herself. She called the ones who stay on the official trail "wusses." Exasperated Heath exclaimed, "If you've hiked all 900 miles of trails in the park, hike them all again in the opposite direction!"

Why did she do it? Why does anyone do it? I understand the allure of hiking off the beaten path, to explore new territory. But, no matter how experienced you are or how well you know the terrain, one slip leading to an injury can be deadly when you are alone where no one else is likely to find you any time soon. Why take that kind of risk? With all her experience, maybe she didn't see it as the risk it turned out to be.

Heath also told us about sixteen-year-old Gabriel Alexander asleep in a hammock in the Hazel Creek area near Fontana Lake on the far end of the park from us. A bear bit him on the head and dragged him from the hammock. The boy's father jumped on the bear and beat on him to get him off his son. Heath pointed out that they still had to hike out and ride their boat across the lake to get help. The boy had severe head and facial wounds.

Heath talked about Jared becoming the lead ranger for the Tennessee side of the park and Will getting the job as acting lead ranger for our quadrant. Heath admired both of them for their competence as rangers. Still, I sensed something in his voice. Will was new to the park and got the position, when Heath was every bit as, if not more, qualified. But then, Heath had not applied for the job. He said he didn't want to be a ranger in the office doing paperwork. He loved his job and that was more important to him than earning extra money.

Camper Windy came to the motorhome to tell us a raccoon was being aggressive in the picnic area. I called dispatch to report it, but had the feeling everyone with a park radio was laughing when they heard me. Bear and elk that's a problem. But a raccoon, that's a joke. Dispatch subsequently reported the aggressive raccoon to Will, but we did not see or hear from him.

We walked to the picnic area to check out the raccoon. Windy had told us that several picnickers had told him the raccoon was climbing on them, apparently looking for food. When we got there, the poor little thing was curled up by a tree next to the creek. It was trembling but looked up when I spoke to it. It did not look very aggressive.

There was a towel on the ground near the tree. When Windy picked it up, the raccoon followed him and his blanket back up to the bridge. We all agreed that he must have been a pet, no longer wanted, and dropped off in the park to fend for himself. When we all stood still, the raccoon sniffed legs and shoes. We had no way to catch it and dared not try to pick it up. So we left the little guy to fend for himself overnight.

Shannon and Will, the UT grad students who were in the group site a few weeks back, were in the parking lot. They said they were looking for a dog sitter. We took Copper to the motorhome while the couple took a hike to the Midnight Hole.

- *"700, Clingman's Dome. It's raining up here, so we are going home. Bye." That was surely a volunteer.*
- *For the first time, I heard dispatch tell a ranger, who was calling in a traffic stop, that he was third in line and there*

might be a delay in getting his information. Then another ranger called in a traffic stop and dispatch said, "You're number four."

- *One ranger called another to be on the lookout for a group of motorcycles. The last one in the group had "dogged" him by going below the speed limit while the rest of the group took off and got far ahead, presumably somewhat above the speed limit. The second ranger said he would take care of them.*

The woman in Site 11 and I admired a beautiful yellow moth on the ladies room wall the next morning. She said she had been an interpretive ranger in Philadelphia and now lived in Asheville, NC. Then she told me she was going to submit a comment card about this campground needing a law enforcement ranger on site. She had been observing the park visitors for the past several days. Ha! Somebody knows what I'm talking about.

Boss Larry dropped by with reservation reports while I was cooking dinner. We told him about the raccoon. He had heard me reporting it and, after hearing our details, decided to call wildlife about it again. Bill Stiver (340) said he would send someone over as soon as he was available. Larry said he was going to look for the raccoon. He came back while we were eating with the raccoon following him. He found it following the Cocke County sheriff down the Big Creek trail. It had apparently followed one group up the trail and another one back down. The maintenance crew from Cosby followed it to our site. It was so adorable that everyone was charmed. When Richard squatted down, the raccoon climbed into his "lap."

Bill Stiver called back later to say that someone would be there in an hour and fifteen minutes. He asked us to keep an eye on the raccoon until the wildlife guy arrived. It was a curious and busy little creature. It was busy inspecting everything including the car tires. He got into a bit of trouble, just like a kitten, when it climbed up into one of our cloth camp chairs and onto the arm, which flipped over and left the little raccoon hanging by its claws. Again, just like a puppy or a kitten, it put its front feet up on the chair getting Andy's attention.

Maybe it smelled something and headed over to the group site to inspect the many coolers and bins. It walked under the long picnic table where the children had dropped bits of food over the past few weeks and sat there chewing on a cheese doodle. Finally, the wildlife guy arrived with two cages. He set them on the ground and was opening a can of sardines. I said, "Come on" to the raccoon and it followed me over to the wildlife guy. He was shocked, "Are you kidding me? That is not a wild raccoon!" He set one trap on either side of the picnic table and baited them with the sardines. The raccoon walked in and the man closed the door behind it. He was amazed how quick it was. He set the raccoon down to go retrieve his other cage. The raccoon was busy eating sardines. When it stopped and turned around to leave, it seemed to realize it was trapped and then, went back to eating more sardines.

- *A child was stung numerous times by yellow jackets. The ranger was standing by to make sure he did not have any serious reactions.*

- *Dispatch called a ranger to say he had the latitude and longitude for a lost party of a woman and three children. The ranger replied that those coordinates put them off trail near the Rainbow Falls Trail. I guess their GPS did not tell them how to get back to the trail. They were not willing to move. The ranger hiked up the trail and found them and was leading them back to the trail, likely with a good educational lecture along the way.*

- *A mother and four children were locked out of the car at the Porter's Creek trailhead.*

- *A ranger called in for a tag and license check for a road rage incident.*

- *At 6:50 dispatch called a ranger to check on a single vehicle accident in the tunnel, blocking one lane. The ranger headed that way. A few minutes later dispatch called to say he had more calls of vehicles getting rear-ended behind the first car. I did not figure out how many cars were involved, but it sounded like a tunnel full. The ranger asked dispatch to call Gatlinburg police to approach from their end of the tunnel. Then dispatch called to say a woman in a mini-van who was rear-ended called from outside the tunnel. A male left the car that hit her and took off on foot, leaving a female in the car. They didn't say whether he was the driver or not. The ranger asked dispatch to forward his description to Sevier County. Pigeon Forge had a canine out looking for the individual on foot. The wrecker could not get through the traffic backup. Some driver's licenses did not come back as valid in the computer system. At 11:10 the ranger asked dispatch to call Gatlinburg and Pigeon Forge to be on the lookout for the man on foot. At 11:42 the ranger reported that they were transporting the female. A man was seen on the spur near a pullout walking toward Pigeon Forge at 11:47 and a ranger was going to make contact. Dispatch said "Pigeon Forge is on the way." They were in foot pursuit at 11:56. At 12:11 Ranger 411 called to say that he was talking with some people who were in the accident event. They said the driver that hit them was intoxicated and gave him a vehicle description. Dispatch was forwarding the information to Pigeon Forge. A bit later, dispatch called Ranger 411 to report that Pigeon Forge had the man in custody and 411 replied that he would meet them at the Pigeon Forge jail.*

- *There was a disabled vehicle at Collins Creek with a child on board. Dispatch called a wrecker to take them back to Cherokee.*

I stayed awake that night worrying about the little raccoon. What are they going to do with him? Would they just let him out somewhere far from a campground? Would he survive in the wild? Larry told us there is a place that takes in wild animals and rehabilitates them somewhere in the region. Would that be animal reform school? Would they be able to teach the little raccoon to survive in the forest?

Spence said he did not do anything on his weekend. As hard as he works during the week, I would think he would really need to rest on his weekend. His split rail fence was knocked down in several places while he was off work. Maybe boulders would be better to line the roads, they just aren't as charming.

We were sitting outside talking to Spence when Andy said, "Baby alert." A man and woman were pushing a baby stroller up the horse trail, and I love babies. Spence took the last drag on his cigarette and got up to nonchalantly throw the butt into the fire ring behind him and take a look. Then he turned around with a stern look and told Andy, "You are going to have to clarify whether you are saying baby alert or babe alert. I got up for nuthin."

Heath stopped by in the evening and asked about the people in the group site. They had not been leaving food unattended. He had been visiting with the old man, Keith, who lives at the entrance to Big Creek and toppled over the side of the road with his horse and buggy. Heath said that Keith seemed depressed. Heath guessed he was "10 beers gone" when he said he was "quittin' the jar."

Heath said he did not come by the day before because he was detailed to accompany the brother of the woman he found dead in the creek to look for her belongings. They found a hiking stick that was not hers, but none of her possessions. That was not a pleasant experience. Heath was just happy that the brother did not want to go back and look any more.

- *At 8:15 dispatch called for a ranger to check the tunnel. Drivers had reported that a man was standing on the top of it over the road. His intentions were not known.*

Sunday was a busy day in Big Creek with cars streaming in all day long. We mostly hung out at the motorhome to reduce our stress level. The only big event was the elk. One of the girls in the group site knocked on our door to tell me a moose was walking up the horse trail. I asked, "You mean an elk?"

"Yes, it's an elk."

I walked up the road from the RV, guessing that she would continue up the horse trail to where it crosses our road. She was calmly nibbling leaves as she walked along. Just as she came out onto the road, she threw her head back, opened her mouth and ran for about five seconds. Then she calmly continued toward the lawn in front of the toilet building. We'd have to tell Spence to keep the grass a little longer for grazing.

Park visitors were gathering in all directions, but she didn't pay much attention to them. She would raise her head periodically to look around at her audience and then continue munching. No one got too close. She was clearly a park elk with tags in both ears and a big tracking collar on her neck. Actually, any elk around there is a park elk. All the others were eaten years ago.

Spence and regular-camper Junior arrived for blueberry cobbler. We were sure Heath would arrive when I pulled the cobbler out of the oven. However, we heard Heath on the radio making a rescue on one of the Cosby trails. When he finished saving the woman, he signed "out of service" at six o'clock.

We saw a huge motorhome in the campground parking lot when we walked around in the evening. The generator and air conditioner were running. The man in Site 1 was rather unhappy about it. He said he came to this campground to avoid generator noise. I put a courtesy note on the windshield to remind them that this is a non-RV campground. I also reminded them that the campground parking lot is for campers only, not that anyone else pays attention to that sign. Andy called it in to dispatch, just in case a ranger might feel inclined to drive to Big Creek.

- *A girl tubing in Deep Creek hit her head on a rock and needed medical attention. The ranger on the scene reported that she was not conscious. Swain County EMS picked up the girl.*

- *A woman called dispatch from the Rainbow Falls trailhead to report that her sixteen-year-old nephew had fallen on the trail and broken his collarbone and perhaps some toes. She had come down the trail ahead of the rest of the party to make the phone call. Ranger 412 went to meet her at the trailhead. Dispatch reported that the 185-pound nephew was about a mile up and hopping down the trail on one foot with the aid of two uncles. After they had been calling around trying to form a litter team, Ranger 412 got to the trailhead, but found no aunt or nephew. Dispatch called the cell phone number and the aunt said he had made it down the trail and they were taking him back to their cabin. They would take him to the hospital later, if necessary. They could have called to let the park know. Several rangers had stayed overtime to be part of the litter team.*

The sun was shining brilliantly when we walked up to the campground in the morning. The mossy boulders along the campground road were giant emeralds.

The little boys from Site 4 were very proud of their new outdoor gear. The whatever-you-call-it was a combination whistle, compass, flashlight, and several other things. They also had new binoculars. The boys were steadily blowing their new whistles. Mom and Dad were taking down the tent while the four kids were hanging around the pickup truck in the parking lot. When we suggested that the parents were going to go absolutely bonkers before they got back to Michigan, they agreed that whistles were probably not the smartest things to buy the boys at that point. We would miss those two families with eight happy children running all over the place.

We were standing at the campground registration board when a man came up and asked if we were rangers. I said, "No, but we can call if you need one." He needed one. He lost two teenagers on the Big Creek Trail. Their group of eight was walking up the trail and the four children walked ahead. When the adults got to the Midnight Hole, only two kids were there. The oldest two had walked ahead of them and passed the Midnight Hole. The parents had waited for a while and then the fathers went looking for them up and down the trail. They had been missing an hour and a half at that point. I called 700 to report. Dispatch asked if Will heard and Will said for Heath to respond.

Andy finished talking to campers who were asking him questions while I walked with the father to the trailhead. I assured him that it is very difficult to get lost in Big Creek; there are steep mountainsides on both sides. We met the mother and the other teens in the parking lot. The mother and I went to the trailhead to wait for Heath. I also assured her that they probably did not get lost. They would have to walk five miles to get to the first trail intersection and it is only 1-1/2 miles to the Midnight Hole and two miles to Mouse Creek Falls. The mountainsides are too steep to go off trail without some effort.

Later, another teen came up and told us she had received a text from the missing teens and they were on the way down the trail with the other parents. I called Heath on the radio and he responded that he was right around the curve and drove up to the trailhead about thirty seconds later. When the missing teens and a set of parents arrived, Heath gave them all some education about hiking in the mountains. Have a plan. Stay together, or wait periodically for the slower hikers. Read the trailhead sign. Think. The athletic young man should have known he walked more than a mile and a half. They said they saw the Midnight Hole and Mouse

Creek falls, but did not know that they were THE hole or THE falls. They are not marked with signs. Heath explained that the national park is preserved wilderness, not your state park. If someone gets hurt on the trail and they are unprepared or don't have a plan, it could take hours or longer before help came. And it would be cold and wet spending the night up there. The parents got just as much of a lecture as the teens. The group thanked Heath and went on their way. Heath leaned against the trailhead sign and struck a Dudley Do-Right of the Mounties pose.

- *Laurel Falls Rover reported that a woman slipped and fell at Laurel Falls. She apparently broke her ankle. Two rangers responded. They carried her out with a chair that only required two people to carry. The woman did not request an ambulance; they would drive to the hospital on their own. A bear was hanging around next to the trail about half way up just to make the rescue more interesting.*

- *A woman slipped and fell on the rocks at the edge of the water in the Chimneys picnic area and could not get up. The initial assessment was that she had broken her leg. Dispatch called for a rescue squad from Gatlinburg to take her to the hospital.*

It was a dark and dreary morning, afternoon, and evening. I must have predicted eminent rain ten times during the day and never went anywhere without my umbrella. It never did rain for real even though I felt a few drops once or twice. I decided to stop forecasting the weather.

It was Monday for Spence and he dropped by for a coffee refill after he had cleaned the toilet building in the horse camp. There is not enough ventilation in the toilet buildings and the walls are always wet with condensation in damp weather. He wiped them down today. The park visitors track in mud and forest debris on the wet floors. After coffee, we headed to the campground and Spence headed to the picnic area toilet building to repeat the cleaning.

- *A ranger asked dispatch if there were any permits for a wedding at the overlook in Cades Cove.*

- *The Cosby campground host called 700 for a ranger to come do a report on a dog-on-dog attack. Heath was up the mountain closing campsite 37. Dispatch then called Will, who was apparently off duty. Then he called a ranger from another region. That ranger said he would go to Cosby when he was finished with what he was doing at that moment. Dispatch called the Cosby host to let her know that it would be sixty to eighty minutes before a ranger would be there.*

Later, I heard Heath on the radio with the rangers who had gone to Cosby for the dog fight. He said he was hiking back to Big Creek with hikers he had evicted from the backcountry sites. He asked the rangers to come pick him up at Big Creek and give him a ride back to his truck, parked at the trailhead in Cosby. I got on the radio and offered Heath a ride, if it would help the other rangers. There was no point in two rangers hanging around for Heath to get off the trail when we could drive him to his ranger truck and the other rangers could go back to their area of the park.

We had quite a storm with plenty of thunder and the usual heavy downpour. Heath knocked on our door soaking wet. I already had the decaf coffee brewed and gave him a cup. Then Andy offered him a slice of leftover Father's Day pizza, which he accepted. What he really wanted was a towel. He dried off his head and then sat on the towel on the sofa. A wide stream of water ran across the floor. He said his boots were full of water. After a short while, there was another knock at the door. It was Walt, a hiker who had come down the mountain with Heath. He was happy to get in out of the rain and drink a cup of coffee too.

They were tired. I offered to drive Walt up to the campground to help him find a campsite. When we got outside, I realized that the family in the group site was still up and asked them if it was all right if he stayed on one of their tent pads, since he was evicted from the backcountry because of a bear. The woman questioned, "Bears?" three or four times. Walt went to the parking lot to get his gear out of his truck. I put another towel on the car seat to help dry the seat of Heath's pants. He loaded his huge soggy backpack into the back seat and sat on the towel in the front seat.

We dropped Heath off at the gate across the trailhead in the Cosby Campground. He said his truck was a ways up and the road was too rough for our car. The rain and fog had cleared off a good bit for the drive back to Big Creek. We were both still wide awake from the evening's adventure when we got back to the motorhome after midnight.

- *The Job Corps center called for a ranger to come make a report. One of the students had stolen the teacher's phone, and she wanted to press charges.*
- *The Cosby Campground Host called for a ranger to come make a report for the bear activity in the campground that morning. It sounded as though the bear was making the rounds of the campsites.*
- *A 48-year-old woman, half way up the trail to Clingman's Dome, was showing signs of a heat stroke. Dispatch called an ambulance. The Clingman's Dome volunteer reported that another woman was on her back beside the trail a bit farther up. She had asthma and needed an inhaler. A third volunteer called in to say she was on her way to direct traffic. The woman with asthma walked out herself and did not want medical assistance. The first woman left in an ambulance.*
- *Richard called dispatch to say that they were having a flash flood in the Cosby Campground. The road was washing out at Rock Creek, normally a tiny stream, on the entrance road. Richard parked his truck across the road to prevent people from attempting to drive through. He said trees had washed down too. A trail crew called in to report they were stuck out on the trail above the Cosby campground because the log bridge was washed out. They were told not to wade across the creek. Later, they said they had walked to the nature trail area to find a log bridge there, but those logs were also washed away. We heard someone say the road was being undercut in the right lane and the road would not be safe for two-way traffic. The underground utilities were exposed. We thought Spence had left for home, but then heard him on the radio directing traffic at Cosby. Heath was over there too and did not come to Big Creek for a bowl of peach cobbler. I never did hear what happened to the trail crew stuck across the creek.*
- *Later, someone reported that a six-foot wall of water was heading down Ramsey Creek in the Greenbrier area. Park personnel headed to the known swimming holes to make sure people got out of the water. The county sent emergency services to make sure people were out of the creek outside the park.*

We went out to check the level of the creek early the next morning and it had gone down. We could hear the folks over in Cosby on the radio dealing with the mess over there. Spence did not show up for coffee, so we figured he was there helping out. We heard Richard on the radio saying they were cutting down hazardous trees in the campground, which was closed.

- *A girl had fallen on the Deep Creek trail and bashed her head open. The reporting party was able to slow the bleeding with pressure. They decided the best way to get her out was to float her down the creek.*

- *A 250-pound 24-year-old man was down off a trail somewhere along the Abram's Creek trail screaming for help. The passerby/reporting party, a firefighter, said he was yelling loudly, but not saying anything except "help." He said they would definitely need ropes to get him out. Later in the evening, we heard that the patient was ambulating out.*

- *Heath reported a multi-vehicle accident on Rt. 321 between Cosby and Gatlinburg with two injuries and a lot of debris on the road.*

We heard Boss Larry on the radio reporting that he was driving someone from Cosby to Big Creek. He came by in the afternoon just as we finished taking down the screen room and packing it into the motorhome. I served him some peach cobbler while we talked. He promised to tell Heath how good it was.

- *A man fell and cut his head and neck at Cataract Falls, near park headquarters. The person calling 700 said there was a lot of blood.*

- *A thirty-foot motorhome was off the road and hanging over a cliff on the Little River Road, near the Townsend "Y." The reporting party said no one was in danger. The husband was walking down the road for help and the wife was with the motorhome.*

Boss Larry told us that he was going to start working three days a week at Elkmont campground on the far side of Gatlinburg. It takes two people to count the money from camping fees and not everyone is authorized to do it. Using campground hosts as witnesses had been banned. I was a little bit offended. Chuck was leaving to take a ranger job on the Blue Ridge Parkway. That left our section of the park with only two rangers, Will and Heath, plus Chase in the backcountry. I figured that meant only one ranger would be on duty four days a week, when the other was off. Big Creek would really be the lawless frontier then. People already did what they damn-well pleased there.

- *Someone reported, "Three llamas off the trail." I didn't get whether the llamas had simply wandered off the trail in search of tasty leaves or whether there was a mishap and they fell off.*

I made a blueberry cobbler for Heath, to make up for the peach cobbler he missed on Monday and Tuesday. Spence and Linda came to clean the toilet buildings and had some cobbler. Spence said he does not like blueberries, but was having seconds just to keep it from Heath. And, he asked me to make sure I told Heath that. Heath did arrive later in the evening. I served him cobbler and gave him the rest to take home. We were still talking when he got a call from dispatch about hikers who had not come off the trail when expected. The caller was at the ranger station. Heath left to talk to him.

We saw Heath's truck in the parking lot with a group of people as we walked to the campground in the morning. There was another missing hiker on the Big Creek trail. We went on to make our campground rounds and Heath was still in the parking lot when we walked back through. All the missing hikers had come off the trail. I said he is a hero and he struck his Dudley Do-Right pose. Heath says that if he takes long enough getting ready to go rescue someone, they walk off the trail before he starts out.

Everyone was getting in their cars when a thin black man with very poor English walked off the trail. He said his friend was hurt up Big Creek trail. He broke his toe and the bone was sticking out. Heath moved his truck to the trailhead and we walked back to our motorhome. We could hear Heath on the radio with dispatch. At first, the injury was worse than he expected and he wanted to get permission to use Spence's Gator to bring the man down the trail. Then he decided that the man could walk well enough. He asked dispatch to get the phone number and address for a hospital ready for him to relay to the party when they got off the trail.

We did a lot of talking with campers, but I was anxious to get back to the motorhome to prepare for leaving the next day. Andy packed up all the exterior things, except the folding chairs. I did laundry all day, including all the park shirts and fleece jackets. I packed up my camp host office and put everything into the car to take to the ranger station.

We had heard Heath on the radio before he arrived. Some hikers had called the park to report that a horse, without a rider, had followed them off the trail. Dispatch called Heath to respond. Horse and rider were eventually reunited and then Heath called in to say he was transporting some hikers to the Big Creek parking lot. We knew we would see him soon.

Heath and Will were supposed to come to pick up money envelopes, but Will got diverted to an ongoing crisis. Heath came alone and told us the rescue on the radio all day was a girl who was a classmate of his oldest son. She decided to climb up Alum Cave bluffs and, at some point, could not go up or down. She spent the night stuck up there. They got her off with a helicopter.

Andy and Heath went to the campground to get the money envelopes out of the iron ranger while I tended the fire. Then, we had coffee and cookies around the campfire on our last evening in Big Creek.

On family vacations, I never wanted to go to the same place twice. Been there, done that. I had the same philosophy when we got the first motorhome. There are so many places to see and we have so little time, going to the same place twice is just inefficient when I want to see it all. So how did we end up returning to Big Creek time after time? One big reason is that Tim, and then Larry, asked us to return the next year just as we were getting ready to leave and feeling a bit sentimental. Another reason is Big Creek is just so beautiful. Staying in the host site there is like having a cabin in the woods, except our cabin is a motorhome. Even though we were sitting still, every day held some new experience: new people, new animals, new flowers, and new stories on the park radio. And, maybe the biggest reason is we gained a new appreciation for the national park people. Of course, we had to go back to see Spence.

According to Ken Burns and the Public Broadcasting Service, the national parks are "America's best idea," but I wouldn't know that from its budget. Apparently, it is not enough to fulfill its mission as the parks rely heavily on volunteers. According to Brent Everitt in the park's Public Affairs Office:

"In fiscal year 2014 (October 2013-September 2014) 2,560 individuals volunteered at Great Smoky Mountains National Park contributing to 150,679 hours. In 2013, the widely-held value estimate for volunteer time was $22.50 [per hour]. This means there was a benefit of over $3.3 million. If we assume each employee works fifty weeks or 2,000 hours a year, that would mean that the 2,560 individual volunteers would equal roughly 75 full-time year round employees."

Is there any other government agency that has so many people willing and even anxious to work for nothing?

Another vital part of the park is the Great Smoky Mountains Association, found on the web at http://www.smokies information.org/. They were established in 1953 to support the park. Their "about" page has a list of some of their remarkable accomplishments and contributions over the years at http:// www. smokiesinformation. org/ info /about-gsma. While you are there, go ahead and click on the "Become a Member" button and then browse the "Official Park Store" to buy some books about the park, its history, flora, and fauna.

There are those who would love to see the national parks be altogether pristine, devoid of traffic, and exist only for those intrepid few who are blessed to know how to deal with backcountry. But that really isn't what the parks are all about.

Wilderness is more of an idea than a reality in America. There are some remote parts of our country that remain virtually untouched. The national parks aren't one of them.

I think the national parks are there to be experienced—by anyone who wants to make the trip. After meeting so many wonderful people, listening to their myriad heartbreaking and uplifting stories, I never ceased to wonder at the magic the national parks hold. As I watched countless people come to enjoy comradery or solitude, to run away or to find themselves, I now know that the national parks are what we make them. They show us parts of ourselves that we may not be proud of—like how we handle ourselves not so well in God's living room. But they can also bring out the very best of who we are—regular folk, wanting to connect to something bigger than ourselves.

As I finish this, I am preparing for yet another summer volunteering at the Great Smoky National Park. I know what I'm in for—too much rain, an overabundance of trash and a few rude, unthinking people. But I also know that I will get exactly what I want—a summer of adventure each and every day, the chance to meet and connect with strangers even if just for a few days, and maybe, just maybe, I'll get lucky and see another bear.

About the Author

Dinata Misovec retired early from database design and development to pursue some life adventures. So far, they have included: living and cruising on a motor yacht; living and traveling in a tiny motorhome in Western Europe; volunteering to teach first graders to speak English; and traveling the United States and Canada visiting national parks, small towns, big cities, and everything in between.

Currently, she and her husband Andy live in the Florida Keys in the winters and all over the rest of the country in the summers. As an avid photographer and blogger, she shares those adventures at www.dinatamisovec.com and on Facebook. Day-by-day photographs of Big Creek are at www.Bigcreek journal.blogspot.com.

The experience as a campground host in the Great Smoky Mountains National Park gave her a new, increased appreciation for the national parks and the people who run and maintain them. She was so surprised, amazed and awed by this experience that she was compelled to share that up-close-and-personal look with a larger audience.

CPSIA information can be obtained
at www.ICGtesting.com
Printed in the USA
BVOW09s0724160617
486874BV00002B/158/P